THE NATIONAL TRUST

Family Handbook

Avebury

The National Trust

Registered Charity No. 205846

Arlington Court

Written by Gillian Osband
Illustrated by Peter Stevenson

First published in 1990
by The National Trust
36 Queen Anne's Gate, London SW1H 9AS

ISBN 0 70780107 9

Designed by Roger Warham
Phototypeset in Monotype Plantin Light 113
by Southern Positives and Negatives (SPAN), Lingfield, Surrey
Printed by Richard Clay Ltd, Bungay, Suffolk

Contents

St Michael's Mount

continued

THE COUNTIES

Introduction

How to use this book

This **Handbook** provides hundreds of ideas for a day out with your family. Ranging from windmills and dovecotes to country houses, gardens and castles, there should be something in the pages which follow to interest even the most choosy member of your family. This book does not include every property owned by the Trust but is a selection of properties judged to be best suited to family visiting.

The entries have been written to appeal to children and give a general idea of the nature of the property, as well as mentioning specific points of interest to look out for. The symbols will give you a quick reference guide to the facilities available. The key to these is on p.11.

Addresses and telephone numbers are given for properties with opening hours wherever possible. For general details of opening arrangements, directions and other practical information relating to the properties we suggest you use the companion volume to this book, **The National Trust Handbook: A Guide for Members and Visitors**. This is updated annually, issued free to all National Trust members and is also available at good bookshops, National Trust shops, or by telephoning Melksham (0225) 705676.

Oxfordshire

Dyrham Park

THE OLDEST HERD OF FALLOW DEER

Facilities for families with babies and small children

Many properties put aside rooms or areas for changing and feeding babies. A symbol 🖉 indicating this facility will appear beside relevant entries. High chairs are also sometimes available in restaurants and tea-rooms, and this facility is indicated by the symbol 🪑. It is advisable to ring the property beforehand to check details.

It is regretted that prams, pushchairs and baby back carriers cannot usually be admitted inside National Trust properties. This is to protect house contents from being damaged unintentionally. However, babies carried in front slings are welcome. Some properties have front carriers for loan to visitors and this facility is shown by the symbol 🧷.

National Trust members are admitted free to properties on presentation of a valid membership card: details of how to join the National Trust are given on p.14. Non-members are required to pay the entrance fee. Children under 5 are admitted free, and accompanied children aged 5 to 17 are normally charged half the adult rate.

Conservation and security measures

Due to the fragile and valuable nature of the contents of many National Trust houses we must ask visitors to observe some restrictions at certain properties. These include limitations on photography, carrying large bags inside houses and a ban on stiletto heels. There are also restrictions on prams, pushchairs and baby back carriers (see note above). These regulations have been introduced after a great deal of research and thought. We hope that you will understand and accept the reasons behind these conservation and security measures.

Dogs

Dogs are not allowed in Trust houses, restaurants and gardens although exceptions are made in the case of guide dogs. Some properties allow dogs on lead in parkland and this is indicated by the symbol 🐕.

Wheelchair access

Although it is rare for a building or garden to be completely accessible to visitors in wheelchairs, the symbol ♿ on appropriate entries indicates places where a reasonable amount of the property can be enjoyed from a wheelchair without undue difficulty. It is advisable to check details of facilities with someone at the property before your visit.

Attingham Park

Family and Under-23 Membership of the National Trust

The National Trust offers a special membership category for families. For £34 a year (1990 rates) the parents and any of their children under 18 are admitted free to National Trust properties on presentation of a valid membership card. Family members receive the **National Trust Magazine** and the **Young National Trust** magazine three times a year as well as the annual **National Trust Handbook** and other literature. Reduced membership with full benefits is also available to young people under 23 for £7.50 a year (1990 rates). Telephone our Membership Department 081-464 1111 for details (code before May 1990 is 01), or complete the form on page 14.

The National Trust and Education

Schools Corporate Membership is available at £40 a year (1990 rates). The card admits a school party of sixty free of charge to not more than one property on the same day. Visits must be booked in advance. Clustering arrangements are available for up to five small primary schools. Telephone our Education Office on 071-222 9251 (code before May 1990 is 01) for details of the scheme and for information about education events at properties.

The Young National Trust Theatre, sponsored by Barclays Bank plc., is the Trust's touring theatre-in-education company which performs with school groups at selected National Trust

Stackpole Estate

properties throughout the season. Telephone the above number for more details or write to the YNTT Administrator, 36 Queen Anne's Gate, London SW1H 9AS.

National Trust Publications for Children

A growing number of National Trust properties offer children's guides and other literature to make the visit more interesting. These properties are indicated by the symbol Ⓐⓐ.

Apart from guidebooks and discovery sheets at properties, the National Trust has a developing children's publishing programme. **Acorn Modern Classics** is a series of novels published in association with Gollancz, based on National Trust properties and written by well-known children's authors. The titles to date are **Blewcoat Boy** by Leon Garfield and **The Children of Charlecote** by Philippa Pearce and Brian Fairfax-Lucy. You may also find **The National Trust Picture Atlas**, published in association with Kingfisher, a useful guide.

There are also four titles in the **National Trust Out and About Activity Book** series published in association with Kingfisher Books. These are **Nature, Castles, Roman Britain** and **Ghosts**. A new series of similar books is planned to be launched in summer 1990 and published by the National Trust. The first two titles in this series of non-fiction paperbacks are **Investigating the Civil War** and **Investigating the Seashore**.

All these books can be bought from good bookshops and National Trust outlets.

Events

S pecial family events are organised at some properties. For further details contact your nearest National Trust Regional Office (see p.12 for addresses and telephone numbers).

Opening times

Most National Trust properties are open between April and October each year. Days and times of opening vary. Full admission details are found in **The National Trust Handbook** which is updated annually.

Please note that not all properties are open on Saturdays. If you are planning a weekend visit it is advisable to check with the property or Handbook. You may, however, like to note that, at the time of going to press, the following properties featured in this book are not normally open on Saturdays.

Sorry-closed on Saturdays

St Michael's Mount (open for special charity days at weekends but NT members have to pay entrance fees)

Sizergh Castle

Townend

Arlington Court (but open Saturdays of Bank Holiday Weekends)

Compton Castle (closed Sunday as well)

Bembridge Windmill (only open Easter Saturday and Saturdays in July and August)

Needles Old Battery

Nether Alderley Mill

Ightham Mote

Greys Court (house closed Saturday)

Hatchlands

Chirk Castle (only open Saturdays in October)

Plas Newydd

Key to symbols

N Adventure playground/play area

] Shop

@ Children's guidebook/publications

. Wheelchair access

P Refreshments

] Children's menu/portions

< Special events

] Animals in park

& Nature trail

] Country/park walks

★ Special exhibitions

⊼ Picnic area

🐕 Dogs on lead in park/country

🐕 No dogs

WC Lavatory

◆ Nappy changing/baby feeding facilities

& Front baby carrying slings available for loan

⊼ High chair in restaurant/tea-room

KEEP OUT! LAST REFUGE OF RED SQUIRREL

Isle of Wight

Useful National Trust Addresses

Headquarters: 36 Queen Anne's Gate, London SW1H 9AS (071-222 9251 – before May 1990 code is 01)
London Information Centre for personal callers: Blewcoat School, 23 Caxton Street, London SW1
Membership PO Box 39, Bromley, Kent BR1 1NH (081-464 1111 – before May 1990 code is 01)

1 Cornwall: Lanhydrock, Bodmin PL30 4DE (Bodmin (0208) 74281-4)

2 Devon: Killerton House, Broadclyst, Exeter EX5 3LE (Exeter (0392) 881691)

3 Wessex: (Avon, Dorset, Somerset, Wiltshire) Stourton, Warminster, Wiltshire BA12 6QD (Bourton, Dorset (0747) 840224)

4 Southern: (Hampshire, the Isle of Wight, South-Western Greater London, Surrey and West Sussex) Polesden Lacey, Dorking, Surrey RH5 6BN (Bookham (0372) 53401)

5 Kent & East Sussex: (includes South-Eastern Greater London) The Estate Office, Scotney Castle, Lamberhurst, Tunbridge Wells, Kent TN3 8JN (Lamberhurst (0892) 890651)

6 East Anglia: (Cambridgeshire, Essex, Norfolk, Suffolk) Blickling, Norwich NR11 6NF (Aylsham (0263) 733471)

7 Thames & Chilterns: (Buckinghamshire, Bedfordshire, Berkshire, Hertfordshire, London north of the Thames, and Oxfordshire) Hughenden Manor, High Wycombe, Bucks HP14 4LA (High Wycombe (0494) 28051)

8 Severn: (Gloucestershire, Hereford & Worcester, Warwickshire, part of West Midlands) Mythe End House, Tewkesbury, Glos GL20 6EB (Tewkesbury (0684) 850051)

9 South Wales: (Dyfed, Gwent, West Glamorgan, southern part of Powys) The King's Head, Bridge Street, Llandeilo, Dyfed SA19 6BN (Llandeilo (0558) 822800)

10 North Wales: (Clwyd, Gwynedd, northern part of Powys) Trinity Square, Llandudno, Gwynedd LL30 2DE (Llandudno (0492) 860123)

11 Mercia: (Cheshire, Merseyside, Shropshire, Greater Manchester, most of Staffordshire, part of West Midlands) Attingham Park, Shrewsbury, Shropshire SY4 4TP (Upton Magna (074 377) 343)

12 East Midlands: (Derbyshire, Leicestershire, Lincolnshire, Northamptonshire, Nottinghamshire, South Humberside, parts of Cheshire, Greater Manchester, Staffordshire, South Yorkshire and West Yorkshire) Clumber Park Stableyard, Worksop, Notts S80 3 (Worksop (0909) 486411)

13 Yorkshire: (includes North, South and West Yorkshire, Cleveland and North Humberside) Goddards, 27 Tadcaster Road, Dringhouses, York YO2 2QG (York (0904) 702021)

14 North-West: (Cumbria and Lancashire) Rothay Holme, Rothay Road, Ambleside, Cumbria LA22 0EJ (Ambleside (05394) 33883)

15 Northumbria: (Durham, Northumberland, and Tyne & Wear) Scots' Gap, Morpeth, Northumberland NE61 4EG (Scots' Gap (067 074) 691)

16 Northern Ireland: Rowallane House, Saintfield, Ballynahinch, Co. Down BT24 7LH (Saintfield (0238) 510721)

Regional Offices

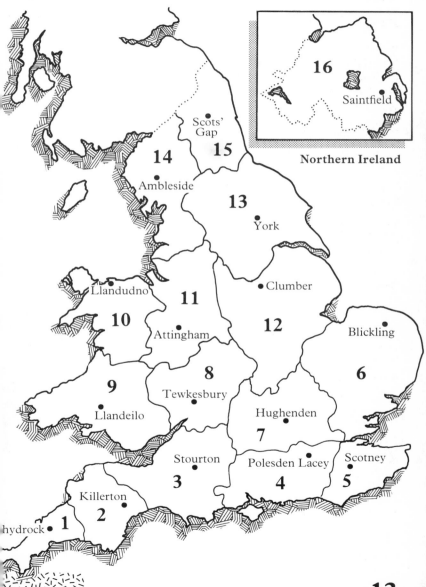

16 Saintfield

Northern Ireland

Scots' Gap

14 Ambleside

15

13 York

Llandudno

11 Clumber

10 Attingham

12 Blickling

8 Tewkesbury

9 Llandeilo

Hughenden

7

Stourton

3 Polesden Lacey

Scotney

4 5

Killerton

hydrock 1 2

Application for Membership

If you join the National Trust you'll receive a card entitling you to free admission to a growing number of the Trust's historic houses, castles, gardens and countryside. You will receive regular mailings of Trust literature including the annual National Trust Handbook, colour magazine and shopping catalogue. Family and under-23 members also receive the Young National Trust Magazine. Above all, your subscription ensures that the Trust will be able to continue its work of preserving the properties under its care for generations to come.

For details of how to join the National Trust and current subscription rates return this form to:

The National Trust
Membership Department
PO Box 39
Bromley
Kent BR1 1NH

Please send me details of how to join the National Trust

Name

Address

Postcode

Read this first ...!

Do you want to visit a gold mine or find a priest's hole? Would you prefer to see a working cotton mill or a farm with rare breeds of animals? If you want ideas for a wonderful day out, look through the pages of **The Family Handbook** and see what the National Trust has to offer. There should be something to interest everyone in the pages which follow.

Knightshayes Court

Now read this ...

When can you visit?

Look in **The National Trust Handbook** for opening times.

How much does it cost?

If you're a National Trust member you get **free** admission to the properties. If you're not, look in **The National Trust Handbook** to find out the entrance fees.

Special Events

Many properties hold special events during the school holidays. To find out what's on, where and when, contact your local National Trust office (see p.12).

Avon

Dolebury Warren

12m S of Bristol, E of A38 above Churchill

*(and under control at lambing time)

Climb to the top of this hill and you'll have a great view of th
Mendips. This is a Site of Special Scientific Interest and has a
unusual combination of heather moorland and limestone grass
land.

Don't Miss...

● The remains of the Iron Age hill fort at the top of the
hill.

● The remains of a Celtic field system.

● The pillow mounds of the rabbit
warrens dating back to
the Middle Ages.

Dyrham Park

Dyrham, near Chippenham SN14 8ER
Tel. Abson (027 582) 2501
8m N of Bath, 12m E of Bristol off A46

The name Dyrham comes from the Saxon word 'Deor-ham
which means deer enclosure, and one of the oldest herds o

fallow deer still roams Dyrham's parkland. The house was built for William Blathwayt, who was William III's acting Secretary of State from 1692 to 1710.

Don't Miss...

- The house was built just after the Glorious Revolution, when William of Orange and his wife, Mary Stuart, came over from Holland to rule England. You can see the Dutch influence on the furnishing of Dyrham. There are leather-hung walls, Dutch paintings and blue-and-white china vases designed for holding tulips. The Balcony Room has door locks and hinges engraved with daffodils and tulips.

- The trick picture by the Dutch artist, Samuel Van Hoogstraeten, which is hung near the Cedar Staircase to make it look as if the house has an extra corridor. Don't try and walk down it...

- There is a statue of Neptune at the top of the hill left over from the time when the house had a fantastic water garden, with waterfalls, terraces and fountains. This was replaced in the eighteenth century by the 260-acre park you see now.

Remember to consult **The National Trust Handbook** for opening times, admission prices and other details.

Bedfordshire

Willington Dovecote and Stables

Willington, near Bedford
4m E of Bedford, N of the A603

Have you ever thought why dovecotes and pigeon houses were built?

In the days before feeding crops were grown in winter, only a few animals could be kept and fed in the cold months. Many animals would be killed and, without deep freezes to keep meat fresh, the only way to preserve it was by thorough salting.

It was the privilege of the Lord of the Manor to build himself pigeon house or dovecote full of nesting boxes – and birds to ry the winter diet. Now the menu could include stuffed geon or dove pie!

This is the history behind Willington Dovecote which was ilt in the sixteenth century by Sir John Gostwick, Cardinal olsey's Master of the Horse.

Don't Miss...

● The huge dovecote is lined with nesting boxes for 1,500 birds. Pigeon pie was obviously a popular dish with Sir John.

● The adjoining stables are unusual because they were built with living quarters and fireplaces for the grooms.

● You have to make an appointment to see inside. Contact Mrs J. Endersby, 21 Chapel Lane, Willington MK44 3QJ (tel. Bedford (0234) 838278).

Berkshire

Basildon Park

ower Basildon, near Reading RG8 9NR
el. Reading (0734) 843040
tween Pangbourne and Streatley, 7m NW of Reading on W side of 329

his elegant Neo-classical house was built for Francis Sykes in 76–83 on his return from India where he had made a fortune orking for the East India Company. It is set in parkland verlooking the River Thames.

Don't Miss...

● The Shell Room is covered in intricate patterns made out of exotic sea and land shells. This was a fashionable way of decorating small rooms in the eighteenth century. There are also other shells on display.

● The house is built with an unusually shaped octagonal room on the ground and first floors.

● There are garden and woodland walks to explore. The pair of stone dogs on the lawn at the back of the house were brought back from Italy in the middle of the nineteenth century.

Buckinghamshire

Boarstall Duck Decoy

Boarstall, near Aylesbury
Tel. Brill (0844) 237488
Midway between Bicester and Thame, 2m W of Brill

♿ ❀ ★ 🐕 WC

This unusual eighteenth-century duck decoy, set in 13 acres of woodland, is still in working order.

Don't Miss...

● The duck decoy works in the following way. The decoy man and his dog are hidden by reed screens beside the decoy pond. The dog runs in and out between the screens arousing the curiosity of the ducks who follow him. They are lured down a channel called a 'pipe' made of net-covered loops over the water and caught at the end of the net.

● The decoy was originally built to catch ducks for food. Any ducks caught now are ringed and numbered to study migration patterns.

● Boarstall's decoy dog, Abingdon, is one of only nine Dutch Kooikerhondje dogs in England and is the breed traditionally used at duck decoys. She was given to the decoy by the Abingdon National Trust Association in May 1989.

● Talks and demonstrations are given regularly by the Warden. Telephone before you go to find out the times.

● There is a nature trail in the woods and an exhibition.

Claydon House

Middle Claydon, near Buckingham MK18 2EY
Tel. Steeple Claydon (029 673) 349/693
In Middle Claydon 13m NW of Aylesbury, 3½m SW of Winslow

In 1620 Edmund Verney, who became Knight Marshal and Standard Bearer to Charles I, was the first member of the family to live at Claydon. The present house was built mainly between 1752 and 1768, and Sir Edmund's descendants still live here.

Don't Miss...

● The inside of the house is richly decorated with extraordinary carvings by the eighteenth-century carver, Luke Lightfoot. The woodwork is crammed with carvings of birds and strange creatures called wyverns – winged, two-legged scaly monsters.

● The Chinese Room is particularly ornate with a whole canopy carved out of wood and decorated with tiny wooden bells.

● The Gamelan – a collection of gongs and xylophones from Java given as a present by Sir Stamford Raffles, the island's lieutenant governor, to Sir Harry Verney in the mid-nineteenth century.

● Florence Nightingale's sister, Frances Parthenope, married Sir Harry Verney and Florence often used to visit Claydon. You can see the bedroom where this pioneering nurse used to sleep and some of her possessions, including letters written during the Crimean War in the mid-nineteenth century.

● Some say that the ghost of Sir Edmund Verney haunts Claydon. He was captured by Cromwell's men at the battle of Edgehill but refused to surrender Charles I's standard, so the Roundheads cut off his hand and killed him. Later in the battle the king won back the standard still gripped in Edmund's hand. The hand was sent back to Claydon for burial but the rest of the body was never found.

Hughenden Manor

High Wycombe HP14 4LA
T. High Wycombe (0494) 32580
N of High Wycombe on W side of A4128

Hughenden Manor was bought in 1847 by the great Victorian politician, Benjamin Disraeli, and it was his home until he died in 1872. The house is in a beautiful setting and it is clear from Disraeli's writings that he loved Hughenden.

Don't Miss...

● The house still contains many of the Prime Minister's papers, books, mementoes, pictures and furniture. Some of the most famous political and society characters of the day visited Disraeli and his wife Mary Anne at Hughenden and portraits of many of these are featured in 'Dizzy's' Gallery of Friendship.

● It is said that Disraeli's ghost has been seen roaming around the house and going down the cellar steps.

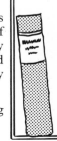

● There are plenty of walks through the grounds and a footpath from the house takes you to the neighbouring Hanging and Flagmore Woods.

Quick Quiz

1. Where in Avon will you find a sleeping rabbit?
2. Where will you find a trick painted corridor?
3. Where can you find exotic sea shells in the Berkshire countryside?
4. Where could you have found a song-bird in a Buckinghamshire stately home?

Answers on page 185

Cambridgeshire

Wicken Fen

Lode Lane, Wicken, Ely CB7 5XP
Tel. Ely (0353) 720274
S of A1123, 3m W of Soham, 9m S of Ely, 17m NE of Cambridge

Wicken Fen is one of the few areas of undrained fenland left i East Anglia. You can get an idea of what the Fens looked lik before the land was drained for agricultural use.

Don't Miss...

● Watch the wardens who look after the fen at work. They carry out the traditional practices of reed, sedge and hay cutting, as well as cleaning ditches and mowing the paths which all help wildlife to flourish.

● There are many wetland plants to look for: purple loosestrife, yellow flag and the rare fen violet and non-stinging nettle! A demonstration garden will help you identify these.

● Quizzes and trails are organised by the education officer in the school holidays.

● In summer the fen is alive with butterflies, dragonflies and other insects. There are over 5,000 species of insect on the fen and it used to be a favourite haunt for Victorian bug hunters, many of whom came out from Cambridge to pursue their studies.

● The fen is home to a variety of birds including the marsh harrier, bittern, great-crested grebe and black tern. There are bird hides so that you can watch the birds unobserved.

● There is a special display in the William Thorpe Building explaining how the fen has developed over hundreds of years.

Wimpole Hall and Wimpole Home Farm

Arrington, Royston, Hertfordshire SG8 0BW
Tel. Cambridge (0223) 207257
8m SW of Cambridge, 6m N of Royston

Wimpole Hall is the largest country house in Cambridgeshire. It is set in 350 acres of parkland, much of which is grazed by animals from Wimpole Home Farm, which was built in 1794 to demonstrate different, exciting new agricultural techniques and breeding stock.

Don't Miss...

● The nineteenth-century stables are home to three enormous Suffolk Punch horses: Nelson, Napoleon and Gedge, looked after by a waggoner. They pull a cart taking visitors to and fro between the Hall and the Farm.

● The Farm is now a rare breeds centre and is a fascinating place to wander round. There are bound to be some strange varieties of farm animals that you've never seen before like Hebridean sheep, Tamworth pigs and long horn cattle.

● The videos about the home farm and farming.

● The children's corner at the Farm and the woodland adventure playground.

● The collection of farming tools, machinery and carts in the Farm's great thatched barn.

● The Gothic Folly in the park was built in 1768 to look like a ruin. There are plenty of footpaths to explore other areas of the park and woodland.

● The house has some very unusual features. Don't miss the eighteenth-century plunge bath which used to hold 2,000 gallons of water and was where the gentlemen would take a dip after a day's hunting.

Cheshire

Dunham Massey

ltrincham WA14 4SJ
el. 061-941 1025
m SW of Altrincham off A56

n the seventeenth century the moated, courtyard house of)unham Massey was owned by the fiercely Protestant Booth amily. Henry Booth was very unpopular with the Catholic King James II and narrowly missed execution for high treason.)n hearing that William of Orange had landed in England in 688 he declared 'I am to choose whether I will be a slave and a apist, or a Protestant and a freeman'. He made the right choice with the Protestant William and Mary on the throne he ecame Privy Councillor, Chancellor of the Exchequer and Earl f Warrington.

Don't Miss...

● The impressive collection of silver which includes a wine fountain and cistern. The handles on the wine cistern are made to look like the boars from the Booth family crest.

● The wooden model of the solar system in the Library.

● There are four remarkable bird's-eye view paintings of the house and park. These were painted in 1750, so the artist would have had to use his imagination to paint what the estate would have looked like from the air. Look out for the portraits of children as you walk round the house.

● The fully-equipped kitchen, laundry and stables.

● The Elizabethan mill in the park was converted to a sawmill in Victorian times. It is still in working order.

● There are walks in the deer park, where you can see the herd of fallow deer and the deer barn, where the animals can shelter in harsh wintry weather.

● Family ticket available.

Remember to consult **The National Trust Handbook** for opening times, admission prices and other details.

Little Moreton Hall

Congleton CW12 4SD
Tel. Congleton (0260) 272018
4m SW of Congleton, on E side of A34

Little Moreton Hall, begun in the late fifteenth century, is one of the most picturesque, moated, timber-framed houses in the country.

Don't Miss...

● The carved detail of the woodwork and variety of pattern on the house's outside walls is very unusual. The original medieval house was extended frequently over the years. See if you can make out which parts are the later additions.

● The north-east corner of the courtyard has messages written in the woodwork which tell us who ordered the extension, when it was built and who the builder was:

God in Al in Al Thing: This windous Whire made by William Moreton in the yeare of our Lorde M.D.LIX.

Richard Dale Carpeder made thies windous by the grac of God.

Spelling has changed a bit since Richard Dale's time!

- The garden has been created to look as Little Moreton Hall's knot garden might have done in the seventeenth century.

- Family ticket available.

Lyme Park

Disley, Stockport SK12 2NX
Tel. Disley (0663) 62023
On S side of A6

The deer at Lyme Park have been famous for centuries. It was the custom to drive the stags across a pond called Stag Pool at midsummer every year. Wild cattle used to roam the park as well. The land was given to the Legh family in 1346 and was their home for the next six hundred years.

Don't Miss...

● Lyme Park is said to be haunted by the ghost of a lady in white. She is Blanche, who died of grief when the corpse of her betrothed was brought back from the Battle of Agincourt in 1415.

● There are paintings of the Lyme Mastiffs all around the house. These huge dogs were bred here since the sixteenth century and were traditionally given as presents to European royalty. Sir Piers Legh II even took his mastiff into battle with him.

● At Lyme the life of Edwardian servants comes alive. Staff dress up to show what daily life would have been like 'below stairs' at the beginning of this century.

● The eighteenth-century Chippendale chairs in the Stag Parlour are covered with material from the red cloak worn by Charles I at his execution.

● There are over 1,300 acres of parkland and moorland to explore. Visit Lyme Cage, a square stone building set high on a ridge in the park. This was a look-out from which people could watch hunting. The cage might also have been used as a place to lock up poachers.

● During the school holidays there are special tours around the house for children.

Mow Cop

m S of Congleton

rom a distance Mow Cop looks like a ruined castle perched igh on its hill. This folly was actually built as a mock ruin for ie local landowner, Randle Wilbraham, in 1754. He used it as a immerhouse.

Don't Miss...

● Mow Cop stands exactly on the boundary between Cheshire and Staffordshire so you can stand with a foot in each county. It also marks the beginning of the Staffordshire Way footpath. You can easily walk the three miles to Little Moreton Hall from here (see p.29).

● It's a steep climb to the top of the hill but the views you get from the summit are worth it. On a clear day you can see across to the Peak District to the east and the Welsh hills to the west.

● The Primitive Methodists held their first meeting here on 31 May 1807. Find the tablet marking this event.

Nether Alderley Mill

Congleton Road, Nether Alderley, Macclesfield
1½m SE of Alderley Edge on E side of A34

There has been a mill on this site since 1290. The present mill was built in the sixteenth century and its two wooden water wheels and machinery were in regular use until 1939.

Don't Miss...

● As the stream was not strong or constant enough to power the wheel, a dam was built so that the water could be stored and fed in at the right pressure.

● The mill is now fully-restored and in working order. Sometimes working demonstrations are given, showing how corn is ground into flour.

● If you have time, visit Alderley Edge. This was once a prehistoric settlement and weapons and pottery from the Bronze Age have been found here. You can now walk along the Edge and get wonderful views over the plain below.

Quarry Bank Mill and Styal Country Park

Wilmslow SK9 4LA
Tel. Wilmslow (0625) 527468
1½m N of Wilmslow off B5166, 2m from M56 exit 5

In 1784, at the height of the Industrial Revolution, a young merchant called Samuel Greg founded a factory mill in the picturesque valley at Styal. The cotton-spinning industry flourished, so by the early nineteenth century an entire village with school, shop and chapel was built for the mill's growing labour force.

Don't Miss...

● The Apprentice House where the children lived. Costumed staff bring alive the day-to-day life of the mill children. Children had to work a 13-hour day, six days a week, in return for food, lodgings and schooling.

- The cotton mill is a living museum where you can see the machines in action and imagine what it would have been like to have been an apprentice, one of the many child workers, employed at Quarry Bank.

- Some of the cottages in the village have been restored to show what the living conditions of an adult mill worker were like.

- The mill is sited in Styal Country Park which has many country walks and footpaths to explore.

- Family ticket available.

Tatton Park

Knutsford WA16 6QN
Tel. Knutsford (0565) 54822/3
3½m N of Knutsford, 4m S of Altrincham

*Toddlers' play area

This imposing house was designed by the architects Samuel and Lewis Wyatt for Lord Egerton at the end of the eighteenth century.

Don't Miss...

- The house has an extraordinary collection of animal heads. They are the big game trophies from the 4th Lord Egerton's hunting trips in Africa and India. He collected so many that he had to build a special hall to display these and other souvenirs of his adventures abroad.

GORILLA

- There are 60 acres of garden to explore including a Japanese garden, a fernery, a rose garden, an orangery and an arboretum.

- The 2,000-acre park is grazed by Soay and Hebridean sheep as well as red and fallow deer. You can also see wild birds on the lake, Tatton Mere.

- Visit the 1930s Home Farm with its livestock and see the steam engine and working dairy.

Cornwall

Countryside

Cornwall has a spectacular coastline and the Trust owns or protects 120 miles of it. There are hair-raising cliff top walks, secret coves, mysterious caves and industrial relics from the county's old tin and copper mines.

● If you're looking for a beautiful beach to visit try one of these: Strangles Beach, near Boscastle, backed by the highest cliff in Cornwall.
The Gannel, Newquay, a beach with lots of wildlife.

● There are also breathtaking cliff top walks at Zennor Head, St Anthony's Head, St Agnes Beacon and Rosemergy and Trerean Cliffs. Look out for the basking sharks at Cape Cornwall – they're vegetarian! But remember, cliffs can be dangerous: keep to the paths, keep dogs on the lead and make sure someone knows where you're going.

● There are lots of villages to visit as well. Hall Walk is a 4-mile trip around the edge of Fowey Harbour. Catch the Bodinnick Car Ferry to start and then enjoy the views of the busy china clay port of Fowey. The walk takes you to the little village of Polruan where you can catch a foot ferry back to Fowey.

● Cornwall's coast can be treacherous as well as beautiful. If you go to Morwenstow, visit the churchyard where the poet-vicar, Robert Hawker, used to bury shipwrecked sailors in the nineteenth century. You can also see the hut he built on the cliff out of driftwood. Try to visit one of Cornwall's unspoilt fishing villages like Mullion Cove on the Lizard peninsula or Port Gaverne on the north coast and sample fish straight out of the sea!

● At the little village of Tintagel, so-called birthplace of King Arthur, you can visit the Old Post Office. This building was built in the fourteenth century to the plan of a medieval manor house, with a large hall. In 1844, four years after Sir Rowland Hill started the penny post, one of the rooms was let out for use as a Letter Receiving Office. It was used as a Post Office for the next fifty years and the room has now been restored to look as it did in Victorian times.

VEGETARIAN BASKING SHARK

Cornish Engines

East Pool and Agar Mine, Pool, near Redruth
Tel. Redruth (0209) 216657
At Pool, 2m W of Redruth on either side of A3047

Long before the Romans came to Britain, tin mining was an important industry in Cornwall and remained so until the end of last century. You can see many remains of the mines around the county. One problem which plagued this industry was that the shafts were very deep and used to flood regularly. However, in 1802 a Cornish engineer, Richard Trevithick, invented a high-pressure steam engine which could pump 2,052 litres of water a minute out of the mines! By 1860 there were 650 of these engines working in Cornwall but when tin was discovered in America and Australia the Cornish tin industry collapsed.

Don't Miss...

● These amazing engines also used to take miners and ore up and down the shafts. Imagine what it would have been like to be a tin miner working hundreds of feet below the surface.

● If you want to see a working engine, contact the Manager at South Crofty Mine; Tel. Redruth (0209) 714821.

● There are many other relics from the tin-mining industry to visit in Cornwall. Just as impressive as the Pool engines (but not in working order) are the mine buildings of Wheal Coates near St Agnes, Levant near Pendeen and Carn Galver near Bosigran.

Cotehele

St Dominick, near Saltash PL12 6TA
Tel. Liskeard (0579) 50434
On W bank of Tamar, 1m W of Calstock by footpath, 6m by road

STEWPOND

Cotehele is one of the most beautiful, romantic and least-altered medieval houses in the country. A great medieval house like Cotehele was more than just a place to live in: when it was built for the Edgcumbe family between 1485 and 1627 it had several roles: fortress, barracks, office, law court *and* hotel! There is also a wonderful estate to explore, showing how the isolated community produced most of its needs.

Don't Miss...

● The peephole in the Gatehouse so that the gatekeeper could keep an eye on what was happening in the courtyard.

● The Retainers' Court used to be the main entrance to the house from a road now covered by the grassy meadow. Look for the arrow slit which was used if visitors weren't friendly!

- There is a large collection of weapons and armour on display.

- Visit the kitchen and see the enormous Tudor hearth with all the hooks for hanging the pots on.

- You can still see in the grounds the medieval dovecote (see p.18 to find out more about dovecotes) and stew pond (for fish) which provided food for the community.

- The River Tamar used to be the main highway for trade and transport. Walk down to Cotehele Quay where you can see *Shamrock*, a restored sailing barge from Victorian times, and the museum.

- The estate workshops are fascinating. See where the estate blacksmith, wheelwright, carpenter and saddler used to work and the fifteenth-century watermill and cider mill.

Lanhydrock

Bodmin PL30 5AD
Tel. Bodmin (0208) 73320
2½m SE of Bodmin, follow signposts from A38 or B3258

*School Resource Pack

Lanhydrock was largely rebuilt after a terrible fire in 1881 destroyed most of the old seventeenth-century house. Valuable books from the library, set up by a chaplain called Hannibal Gammon, were saved by throwing them on to the lawn below; for many years blades of grass were still being found in them as a reminder of the fire.

Don't Miss...

- See what life 'below stairs' was like for a Victorian servant. There is a marvellously equipped kitchen, a game larder, fish larder, meat larder, bakehouse, tiled dairy and many other reminders of day-to-day household life in the late nineteenth century.

- Find the different ways the family ensured that the house would never be destroyed again by fire.

- The rooms in the main house show the comfortable life enjoyed by the owners of Lanhydrock. Make sure you see the Billiard Room.

- If you telephone the house in advance you can arrange to look through and handle boxes of Victorian household objects.

- There are always lots of events organised at Lanhydrock during the school holidays. Telephone to find out what's on.

- There are acres of beautiful grounds to explore.

St Michael's Mount

Marazion, near Penzance TR17 0HT
Tel. Penzance (0736) 710507
Access by foot over causeway at low tide ½m S of A394 at Marazion. Ferry in summer months.

*School Resource Pack
NB The causeway and paths on the island are cobbled and not suitable for wheelchairs, prams and pushchairs.

The cluster of monastic and defensive buildings hugging this island rock form one of the most memorable places to visit in England. The island has been associated with Christianity ever

40

...since the fifth century when it is said that St Michael appeared to a group of fishermen on the Mount. As well as being a place of pilgrimage, the Mount is a stronghold which has played an important role in Cornwall's history.

Don't Miss...

● The Mount is said to have been built by a giant called Cormoran. Find out more about this in the story of *Jack the Giant Killer* and ask to be shown the well, half-way up the hill, into which the giant fell.

● The only way to get to the island is by foot across the causeway at low tide or by ferry at high tide.

● A Benedictine priory was established on the Mount in the twelfth century, and in 1425 the Mount became a manned fortress for two centuries. Walk along the ramparts and see the gun batteries and a sentry box in the old fortifications as a reminder of this time.

● The Mount has many secrets. Visit the church, built on the highest point of the island. When renovation work was being carried out on it in the last century a small dungeon was found containing the skeleton of a man over 7 feet tall!

- Explore the harbour and village. Until recently this was a trading market for Cornish tin and other goods. There are bollards on the waterside made from the barrels of old guns left over from the Napoleonic Wars at the beginning of the nineteenth century.

- Family ticket available.

Trelissick Garden

Feock, near Truro TR3 6QL
Tel. Truro (0872) 862090
4m S of Truro, both sides of B3289

🖼️ ♿ ☕ 📷 ⭐ 🐑 🍁 🚶 ⭐ 🐕 WC 🅰️*

*School resource pack

In June 1583 a brave English navigator, Sir Humphrey Gilbert set sail from Plymouth in his frigate the *Squirrel*. He discovered Newfoundland but on the return voyage to England his ship sank and he was drowned. Hundreds of years later Sir Humphrey's descendants settled at Trelissick, and when John Davies Gilbert built the estate water tower in 1865 he crowned it with a squirrel weather-vane. When a south wind blows the squirrel faces out to sea where the ship bearing the same name made history.

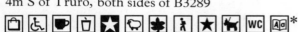

Don't Miss...

● Trelissick House is not open but its grounds are marvellous to explore. Follow the nature trail in the woods or discover the garden's huge variety of plants which have been collected from all over the world.

● There is a woodland walk which runs along the banks of the River Fal past the King Harry Ferry and the berths where redundant merchant ships are laid up. This area, with all its quiet inlets, used to be popular with smugglers.

˙rerice

˙stle Mill, near Newquay TR8 4PG
˙l. Newquay (0637) 875404
˙ SE of Newquay via A392 and A3058

˙iis secluded manor house was rebuilt in 1572 for one of the ˙eat families of Cornwall, the Arundells. It is tucked away in ˙e countryside just outside the busy resort of Newquay and ˙en you visit Trerice you step back into the past.

Don't Miss...

● Find the two Arundell lions carved in granite guarding the path to the front door.

● Look for other clues to the ownership of the Arundell family. The centre panel of the plasterwork ceiling in the Hall has the initials of Sir John Arundell, his first wife Katherine and his sister Margaret.

● At the back of the house are the old farm buildings. The great barn dates back to the fifteenth century and if you go up to the hayloft above the stables you'll see probably the only lawnmower museum in the world! There are lawnmowers of every shape and size including some which were horse-driven. You can even see special soft shoes made for the horses so that the newly-mown turf was not damaged by their hooves.

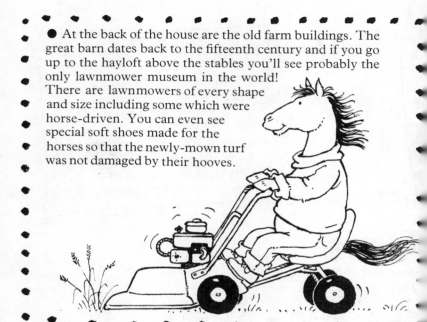

Quick Quiz

Unscramble these words to find six Cornish properties.

1. Reilsticks Rednag.
2. Dahlcornky.
3. Honcris Sneenig.
4. Trewwormons.
5. Reetirc.
6. Leethoce.

Answers on page 185

Cumbria

Countryside

The Lake District, one of the most beautiful areas of Britain, has been threatened by development and tourism for two hundred years. Inspired by the poet William Wordsworth who loved the area, a campaign was waged to protect the Lake District. In particular the fight was taken up by the fiery Canon Hardwicke Rawnsley, one of the founders of the National Trust, and a determined woman, Mrs Heelis, better known to us as Beatrix Potter.

As a result today a quarter of the Lake District is owned or protected by the National Trust. But there is always work to do repairing the wear and tear on the area's roads, footpaths and lake shores.

It is wonderful place if you like the outdoors. There are calm lakes, quiet valleys and breathtaking mountains. Unfortunately there is only room in this book to suggest a few places to visit.

● Buttermere valley with the lakes of Buttermere, Crummock Water and Loweswater where you can hire boats and fish. See Scale Force, the highest waterfall in the district, at the south end of Crummock Water.

● Wasdale is probably the wildest of the valleys and contains Scafell Pike, England's highest mountain, and Wastwater, the deepest lake.

● Coniston Water: take a ride in *Gondola* (tel. Coniston (053 94) 41288) the Trust's restored Victorian steam yacht, and visit the village of Hawkshead and the Beatrix Potter Gallery (see p.46).

● Ullswater: climb up and see the 65ft waterfall of Aira Force.

Windermere: visit the tiny Bridge House at Ambleside which was once home for a family of eight!

Beatrix Potter Gallery

Main Street, Hawkshead LA22 0NZ
Tel. Hawkshead (09666) 355
In Hawkshead, next to the Red Lion Inn

*nearby
NB Gallery not suitable for prams, pushchairs and baby back packs

Tom Kitten, Jemima Puddleduck and Mrs Tiggywinkle... you
can now see Beatrix Potter's original paintings of many of the
characters from her books on show at this gallery. For conservation reasons only a selection of the paintings and drawings can
be displayed at a time, but you'll still get a glimpse into the
world Beatrix Potter created.

Don't Miss...

● Beatrix Potter was a skilled artist and
you can see here her realistic drawings
of the animals and countryside of her
beloved Lake District.

● The building used to be the office
of her husband William Heelis, a
solicitor, and has been kept as he would
have known it.

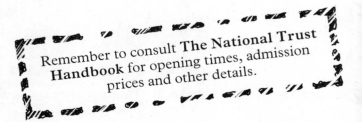

Remember to consult **The National Trust Handbook** for opening times, admission prices and other details.

Hill Top

Near Sawrey, Ambleside LA22 0LF
Tel. Hawkhead (09666) 269
In S of Hawkshead at Near Sawrey behind the Tower Bank Arms

 * ![] [WC]

At Tower Bank Arms next door

Beatrix Potter bought this small farm in 1905 with the profits from her first book *The Tale of Peter Rabbit*. By the time she died she had bought fourteen upland farms and had saved 4,000 acres of fell land. She left it all to the National Trust.

Don't Miss...

● Beatrix Potter wrote and illustrated many of her books at Hill Top and the farmhouse has hardly changed from that time. You can see the rooms where she used to work.

● She was also an experienced farmer and devoted much of her time to breeding prize-winning Herdwick sheep. Look out for this hardy breed of sheep on the hills. Some have been known to survive for up to a month under snow drifts by eating the fleece off their backs!

● The garden has been laid out to look like Mr Mac-Gregor's garden with a vegetable patch to tempt Peter Rabbit.

● Hill Top has a great problem. It is so popular with visitors that it almost bursts at the seams on Bank Holiday weekends and during school holidays. If you can, visit Hill Top outside these times and try to be there early in the day.

Sizergh Castle

Near Kendal LA8 8AE
Tel. Sedgwick (053 95) 60070
3½m S of Kendal

The Strickland family have owned Sizergh since 1239 but th
site was probably inhabited and fortified long before it came t
the family.

Don't Miss...

● One of the oldest parts of Sizergh Castle, the Pele Tower, was built in the fourteenth century. The tower is the largest in the country and was built as a defence against the raiding Scots.

● See the old winding staircase with its sharp turns to the right. This made it very difficult for an attacker to wield his sword.

● The Strickland family were strong Catholics and Stuart supporters. You can see many Stuart portraits and royal relics in the house, like the silk and gold bedspread belonging to James II. When James II was forced to flee England in 1688, Sir Thomas Strickland refused to abandon his king and went with him to France.

● The window seat at the top of the Pele Tower has remained unchanged for about 600 years. The ladies of the house would have once sat here, sewing and spinning and looking down on the bustling scene below – part farmyard and part barracks.

Townend

Near Troutbeck, Windermere LA23 1LB
Tel. Ambleside (053 94) 32628
m SE of Ambleside at S end of village

B Not suitable for prams, pushchairs and baby back packs

The Browne family who lived at Townend for over four
centuries were what is called 'statesman farmers'. This doesn't
mean that they were politicians, but that they were moderately
wealthy farmers working their own land. Their seventeenth-
century farmhouse is crammed with their everyday furniture
and possessions and gives a good idea of what life was like for a
statesman farming family.

Don't Miss...

MRS BROWNE MAKING A SHOPPING LIST.

● The Brownes personalised
much of their furniture by
carving patterns, dates and
heraldry on it.

● The family was also unusually
meticulous in keeping records of
everything – receipts, bills,
shopping lists and farm details – so
we know a great deal about their
everyday affairs.

● The long oak table in
the firehouse, or main
room, was where the
Brownes, the farmhands
and servants would have
eaten all their meals together.

Wordsworth House

Main Street, Cockermouth CA13 9RX
Tel. Cockermouth (0900) 824805
Main Street, Cockermouth

NB Not suitable for prams, pushchairs and baby back packs

William Wordsworth, one of England's greatest poets, was born
in this house in April 1770. Many of his poems were inspired by
the beauty of the Lake District. He spent eight happy years in
this Georgian house with his three brothers and his adored
sister, Dorothy. They used to play in the large garden and hunt
for bird nests along the garden terrace.

Don't Miss...

● You can play hide-and-seek on the terrace or in the
garden just as Wordsworth did with his brothers and sister.

● There is a video display in the old stables where you can
find out more about the poet and his life.

Derbyshire

Countryside

Derbyshire has gentle river valleys, pastures and woodlands as well as the high peat moorlands and towering crags of the peaks. Most of the land protected by the Trust in Derbyshire and its neighbouring counties of Staffordshire and South Yorkshire are in the Peak District National Park. There are many walks to take, peaks to climb, and plenty of wildlife to look out for. Here are a few places to visit:

Hope Woodlands – 16,500 acres of lonely, dramatic moorland crossed by the Pennine Way.

Dovedale is internationally famous for its ash woods and remarkable geological formations. Don't miss Jacob's Ladder and the Towering Twelve Apostles.

From Alport Height you can see across half of Derbyshire and the width of Staffordshire.

Mam Tor in Edale is known as the 'shivering mountain' because it has suffered from so many landslips over the centuries. On its summit is a huge Iron Age hill fort with magnificent views.

Kinder Scout, 2,000 feet above sea level, on the High Peak Estate is probably the most famous landmark in the Peak District. It is known not only for its striking scenery but also because in 1932 a group of ramblers held a mass trespass there, campaigning for the right of access to privately owned uplands.

Remember: When you go walking on moorland or climb peaks, you must be properly equipped. Have good walking shoes or boots, waterproof and warm clothing, an Ordnance Survey map and some food. Let someone know where you are going.

●In 1665 the Plague came to Eyam when the village tailor received a parcel of cloth from London, infested with plague carrying fleas. When the villagers found out, they made a brave decision: no one was allowed in or out of the village until the infection had burnt itself out. Over three-quarters of the villagers died as a result. The Riley Graves are a reminder of the tragic story of seven members of the Hancock family who died of the plague in one week during August 1665. You can see the graves at Righ Lea Meadow just outside Eyam Village.

Calke Abbey

Ticknall DE7 1LE
Tel. Derby (0332) 863822
9m S of Derby, on A514 at Ticknall between Swadlincote and Melbourne

Calke has been owned by the same family, the Harpur Crewes, for hundreds of years. The fascinating thing about Calke is that the family never seemed to throw anything away and the house is crammed with possessions collected over the years.

Don't Miss...

● In 1886 Sir Vauncey Harpur Crewe inherited the house. He was an extraordinary recluse, obsessed with collecting objects of natural history. The house is full of stuffed animals and his collections of geological specimens, eggs and butterflies; there is even an alligator skull...

● A state bed hung with embroidered Chinese silk arrived at Calke in the eighteenth century but was never unpacked from its cases! As a result the old silk has not faded or rotted with age and light. The bed has now been assembled and is on display behind glass to protect it.

● The old kitchen has not been altered since it was abandoned in 1928. Imagine what it was like to be a servant working there.

● There is a collection of carriages in the stable yard – Sir Vauncey banned motor vehicles on his estate. Make sure you see the tackroom, with its display of saddles and harnesses.

● There are deer in the park and also a flock of rare Portland sheep. This breed is said to have come to England with the Spanish Armada in the sixteenth century, when the sheep swam ashore from the wrecked ships.

● The walled garden is worth exploring. This used to contain the flower garden, the physic garden (originally for growing herbs for medicines) and the kitchen garden. You can see the gardener's bothy with the cabinet for keeping different varieties of seed. And find out what an auricula theatre is...

Bess, building Hardwick Hall.

Hardwick Hall

Doe Lea, Chesterfield S44 5QJ
Tel. Chesterfield (0246) 850430
6½m W of Mansfield on A617

Hardwick Hall is one of the greatest houses in England. It stands dramatically on the crest of a ridge and, as you approach, you can see, set along the roofline, the initials of the woman who built it, Elizabeth Shrewsbury, better known as Bess of Hardwick.

Born about 1520, this energetic and ambitious daughter of a country squire became one of the richest women in England. She married and outlived four husbands, each time increasing her social position and wealth. When her last husband died in 1590 Bess found herself even richer than before and set about building a splendid house, next to her childhood home. She was then almost 70 years old but she drove the workmen with great energy and supervised the building work. The house and its furnishings were not finished until 1597 but Bess still managed to spend her last nine years there.

Don't Miss...

● The magnificent tapestries and needlework all over the house. Most of these tell stories so have a good look at them and try to work out what is going on.

● There is a wonderful table in the High Great Chamber which was probably made to celebrate Bess's marriage to the Earl of Shrewsbury in 1568. It is decorated with a complicated inlay pattern of musical instruments, playing cards, board games and even a sheet of music!

● The kitchen is filled with hundreds of eighteenth- and nineteenth-century brass pots and pans. There is also a mechanical spit and a huge open fireplace to see.

● Once you've seen the house and garden, explore the country park where you can see long horn cattle and white-faced woodland sheep.

Longshaw Estate

Sheffield S11 7TZ
Tel. Hope Valley (0433) 31708
½m from Sheffield, next to A625

This estate covers 1,700 acres of wild and remote countryside in the Peak District.

Don't Miss...

● The traces of village settlements at Lawrence Field and Sheffield Plantation with the remains of defensive stone walls and hut sites.

- The abandoned quarries at Bolehill which used to supply millstones for the local watermills. You'll find old millstones still lying there.

- Some ancient oak forest still survives on the estate, with interesting plants and wildlife.

Sudbury Hall

Sudbury DE6 5HT
Tel. Sudbury (028 378) 305
6m E of Uttoxeter off A50

Baby back packs allowed in museum but not in house

In 1660, a year after he had inherited the Sudbury Estate, George Vernon started building Sudbury Hall. When the house was finished, forty years later, it contained some of the richest decoration in the county, executed by top-class craftsmen brought from London.

Don't Miss...

- The wood carvings were mostly done by Edward Pearce and Grinling Gibbons. The staircase is decorated with realistic baskets of fruit while the Drawing Room fireplace is covered with carvings of fish and birds. The plasterwork in the house is just as lively.

- If you're feeling adventurous you can climb the chimney!

GRINLING GIBBONS

● The Museum of Childhood in the servants' quarters has a wonderful collection of toys from the past, a display of the sort of clothes children used to wear and an exhibition on children in history.

● The Victorian schoolroom is still used by school parties to find out what it was like to be a student a hundred years ago.

Devon

Countryside

Over 76 miles of Devon's coastline is under the Trust's protection. It's a wonderful area to explore, with secret coves and beaches linked to tales of smugglers and wreckers. Devon also has beautiful country inland. Here are just a few of the Trust's places to visit.

● Bolt Tail to Overbecks – south coast, near Salcombe with 6 miles of rugged coastline to walk along. Pass Bolt Tail Camp, a promontory fort; watch the seabirds at Bolt Head and Bolt Tail; walk down to Soar Mill Cove and Starehole Bay and have a swim and explore the shoreline; stop off at Overbecks Museum (see p.66) with its unusual collections; walk to Salcombe Harbour and watch the boats.

● Portlemouth Down and Prawle Point – on the east side of Salcombe Harbour, where there are 330 acres of low cliffs with walks, views and sandy coves. Either take the high path along the cliffs or one which follows the shore.

● Wembury Bay – on the south coast, 6 miles east of Plymouth. A good beach. You can have tea at the old mill which is now used as a beach café with the old millstones as tables.

● Branscombe and Salcombe Regis – a 4-mile cliff walk from Branscombe Mouth to Dunscombe Cliff. Below are good beaches best reached at Branscombe and Weston Mouths. At Branscombe village you can see thatched cottages, a forge and a bakery where you can still visit the old bakeroom and stop for a cup of tea.

● Lee to Croyde – there are wonderful cliff walks along this stretch of the north coast. At Baggy Point you may be lucky enough to find prehistoric flints. There are beaches and sand dunes at Woolacombe. Look out for standing stones at Damage Cliffs and Woolacombe Barton.

● Clovelly to Mortland Point – a spectacular coastal footpath from which you can walk down over 400 steps to Shipload Bay to see the seals which regularly pop their heads out of the water. There is a nature reserve at the Brownshams, near two ancient farmhouses owned by the Trust.

● Trowlesworthy Warrens – where rabbits used to be bred in medieval times for their meat and fur. The small and ancient farm here was originally the house of the warrener, whose job it was to look after the rabbits.

Arlington Court

Arlington, near Barnstaple EX31 4LP
Tel. Barnstaple (0271) 850296
7m NE of Barnstaple on A39

Arlington Court was built for Colonel John Chichester in 1820 as his family home. The building now houses hundreds of fascinating objects collected by Miss Rosalie Chichester, the last member of the family to live at Arlington.

Don't Miss...

● Rosalie travelled widely and brought souvenirs home from all over the world which are now on display through the house. There are model ships, shells and collections of old furniture.

● In the stables there is a collection of carriages and carts of all shapes and sizes designed to be pulled by anything from a horse to a dog. Sometimes these carriages are put into action and rides are available – telephone to find out more.

● The house is set in a park where you can see Shetland ponies, Jacob sheep and peacocks. There are also woodland walks and a lake.

Buckland Abbey

Yelverton PL20 6EY
Tel. Yelverton (0822) 853607
6m S of Tavistock, 11m N of Plymouth off A386

Buckland Abbey was the home of Sir Francis Drake, the famous sixteenth-century naval commander and explorer. If you're interested in naval history, it's a must to visit.

Don't Miss...

● The display in the Long Gallery outlines the history of the abbey before it was converted into a house by Drake's old rival, Sir Richard Grenville.

● The Drake Gallery contains fascinating relics connected with the famous seafarer. There are flags which may have flown on his ship, the *Golden Hind*, when he sailed around the world from 1577 to 1580; there are also documents with detailed accounts about the Armada and medals struck to commemorate the event.

● You can also see Drake's Drum which, according to legend, will start to beat if England is ever in danger.

● It is said that Drake sold his soul to the Devil in exchange for help to destroy the Spanish Armada. Some say they have seen Drake's ghost driving across Dartmoor in a black coach drawn by four headless horses, accompanied by twelve goblins and a pack of baying hounds!

● The Tudor kitchen is fitted out with equipment from days gone by when hams and bacon sides would hang from the ceiling. The antlers on the wall are rumoured to be from a stag which once chased Sir Francis Drake up a tree. He took his revenge by shooting the animal and mounting the antlers!

● Because Buckland was once an abbey it has one of the largest tithe barns in the country, and the old monastic ox sheds are now hired out to craftsmen whom you can watch at work.

● The monks' guesthouse has been restored and now houses an exhibition on monastic life at Buckland.

Castle Drogo

Drewsteignton EX6 6PB
Tel. Chagford (06473) 3306
4m S of A30 Exeter to Okehampton road

Julius Drewe was a millionaire by the time he retired at the age of 33 in 1889. Convinced that he was descended from a Norman baron, Drewe was determined to build a huge country house to reflect his wealth and ancestry. Castle Drogo, designed by the most famous architect of the day, Sir Edwin Lutyens, is the result of his dream.

Don't Miss...

● Castle Drogo has all the features a 'real' castle should have: 6-foot thick walls, arrow slits *and* a working portcullis. There is an exhibition in the Gun Room on the building of the castle.

● The Drewe Lion, the family's heraldic symbol, can be seen all over the house.

● Lutyens, like Robert Adam before him, designed many of the contents of the building as well, even kitchen implements.

● The tower bathroom has an elaborate range of controls for the shower.

● The gardens were also designed by Lutyens and the strong geometrical designs are carried through here as well. There is a huge circular croquet lawn – you can hire the equipment from the shop and have a game.

Compton Castle

Maridon, Paignton TQ3 1TA
Tel. Paignton (0803) 872112
At Compton, 4m W of Torquay, 1m N of Marldon

*in Castle Barton

This fortified manor house, with its curtain wall, watchtowe and portcullis entrance, was and still is the home of the Gilber family and their descendants. The three Gilbert boys born in the mid-sixteenth century all became famous for their seafarin actions: John was a vice-admiral and helped to defeat th Spanish Armada; while his younger brothers Humphrey an Adrian were explorers... and their half-brother was Walte Raleigh!

Don't Miss...

● This castle was built between the fourteenth and sixteenth centuries and was probably fortified during the mid-sixteenth century to protect the family from isolated raids by Frenchmen sailing across the Channel.

● Look for the squint hole at the entrance to the castle: you needed to check who you were letting in before opening the door.

● One of the famous Gilberts who lived here was Sir Humphrey, the explorer who discovered Newfoundland in 1583 (see the entry on Trelissick). The ends of the pews in the chapel are carved with squirrels, after the name of Sir Humphrey's ship, which sank on the journey home, drowning all the crew.

Killerton

Broadclyst, Exeter EX5 3LE
Tel. Exeter (0392) 881345
On W side of Exeter-Cullompton road (B3181)

When the Killerton Estate, owned by the Acland family since the Civil War, came to the Trust in 1944 it included two chapels, 6,388 acres of farm and woodland, a 300-acre park, 2 villages, 2 hamlets and Killerton House!

Don't Miss...

● The collection of costumes on display in the house dating from the eighteenth century to the present day.

● Killerton garden is famous for its rare trees and shrubs, many of which were brought back from all over the world by nineteenth-century plant hunters.

● Look in the grounds for the Ice House which was large enough to hold two or three years' supply of ice from frozen ponds on the estate.

● Find the Bear's Hut, once the home of a black bear, a family pet. The island in the garden pond used to be a duck refuge but later became the burial ground for other less exotic family pets!

● Climb up to the Iron Age hill fort sited on top of a hill in the grounds.

Knightshayes Court

Bolham, Tiverton EX16 7RQ
Tel. Tiverton (0884) 254665
2m N of Tiverton off A396

Knightshayes Court is a grand Victorian country house desig
ned to look very much older – like a medieval building.

When you're dealing with old houses, hidden secrets can po
up out of the blue! In 1980 a box was found containin
architectural drawings of the house. One sketch showed part of
blue and gold moulded ceiling in the Drawing Room which wa
nothing like the ceiling at the time. A tiny hole was cut in th
plaster which revealed the original ceiling as it appeared in th
drawing. Fifteen plaster panels were taken down and a sheet o
paper was found with the names of the five workmen who wer
ordered to cover the ceiling up on 12 September 1889. Now th
room looks as it would have done 100 years ago.

Don't Miss...

● Other rooms in the house have been restored to their
former glory, including the Billiard Room. The room has
the original Victorian table, cue and balls. There is even a
frieze of billiard balls carved in the stone around the room.

● There are animals carved in some of the house's wooden
beams: find the badger, fox and otter.

● There is a large garden to explore with many rare trees
and shrubs. Make sure you see the topiary with five hounds
chasing a fox sculpted out of a yew hedge. It is said that
once a gardener cut a hole at the end of the hedge so that the
fox could escape!

Lundy

Bristol Channel EX39 2LY
Tel. Ilfracombe (0271) 870870
11m N of Hartland Point

This unspoilt island is famous for its magnificent rocky coast and its birdlife. It was also once a favourite haunt for smugglers. Lundy is now leased to the Landmark Trust which has restored its buildings, many of which can be rented for holiday accommodation.

Don't Miss...

● There is a regular boat service from Bideford and Ilfracombe. Be prepared to walk when you reach the island – cars are banned!

● Lundy means 'Puffin Island' in Norse. You may be lucky enough to see some puffins with their brightly coloured beaks on the cliffs. Look out for other birdlife and the wild soay sheep and sika deer which live on the island.

● Visit Marisco Castle, built in the thirteenth century.

● Walk up to the Old Light, an out-of-service nineteenth-century lighthouse standing on Lundy's highest point. The fogs on the Bristol Channel were so thick that ships couldn't see the beam from the lighthouse which was set too high, so two replacement lighthouses were built low down at each end of the island.

Remember to consult **The National Trust Handbook** for opening times, admission prices and other details.

Lydford Gorge

The Stables, Lydford Gorge, Lydford, near Okehampton EX20 4BI
Tel. Lydford (082 282) 441/320
At W end of Lydford village, halfway between Okehampton an
Tavistock, 1m W of A386

[icons]

Lydford Gorge is a 1½-mile long ravine scooped out by the Rive
Lyd, and has an exciting series of potholes including the Devil'
Cauldron.

Don't Miss...

- You can walk alongside the gorge and 'walk the plank' over the Devil's Cauldron.
- Once through the gorge, the river emerges into an oak-wooded valley. There is a riverside walk along this section which leads to the White Lady waterfall with its drop of 90 feet.

Overbecks Museum and Garden

Sharpitor, Salcombe TQ8 8LW
Tel. Salcombe (054 884) 2893
1½m SW of Salcombe

Overbecks is an elegant Edwardian house in a beautiful setting
and is packed with extraordinary collections of objects. It even
has a secret room...

Don't Miss...

● Can you solve the secret clue? All children who visit the house are given a clue to help them find the house's secret room, crammed with toys and dolls.

● The rest of the house is packed  with odd things to look at: sharks' teeth, model boats, shipbuilding tools, exotic shells, birds' eggs, butterflies and insects. There is even a crocodile skull!

● Ask for a tune to be played on the polyphon, a huge old-fashioned record player.

● Otto Overbeck, a scientist, lived here earlier this century. There is a cabinet showing some of his inventions, including his 'popular rejuvenator' which was supposed to make people feel younger... by giving them an electric shock!

● There is a large garden with wonderful views over the Salcombe Estuary. Because the weather is so mild, palm trees, olives and even banana trees grow here.

Parke

Haytor Road, Bovey Tracey TQ13 9JQ
Tel. Bovey Tracey (0626) 833909
Just W of Bovey Tracey on N side of B3344 to Manton

There are over 200 acres of parkland to explore at Parke which is on the edge of Dartmoor. There is also a Rare Breeds Farm to visit.

Don't Miss...

● The farm with its rare breeds of horses, cattle, pigs, sheep and poultry. There are farm trails to follow, a display on the history of farming, and an unusual collection of model pigs! There is also a pets corner and play area.

● The park has lots of footpaths to follow. You can even walk along a disused railway line.

Saltram

Plympton, Plymouth PL7 3UH
Tel. Plymouth (0752) 336546
2m W of Plympton, 3½m E of Plymouth City Centre

This grand house was transformed by the eighteenth-century architect/designer, Robert Adam.

Don't Miss...

● Adam was an architect with a difference: instead of building a house and letting the owner fill it as he wanted, Adam would design furniture, carpets, ceiling patterns, plasterwork, fireplaces and even doorknobs so that the entire room was planned as a whole. Often his carpets would mirror the design of the ceiling. Every piece of furniture would have a proper place in the room!

● There are fourteen paintings by the famous eighteenth-century artist, Sir Joshua Reynolds. He lived close by and often used to visit the house.

● Three rooms at Saltram are covered in very rare eighteenth-century Chinese wallpaper. The Chinese style, chinoiserie, was very popular at the time. The sailing ships bringing Chinese porcelain and tea to Britain would have carried wallpaper too. If you look carefully you can make out cut-out butterflies and birds provided by the Chinese to cover up the joins – but don't touch, the wallpaper is very fragile.

● The old kitchen looks like it would have done in the eighteenth-century with its copper pans, strange cooking gadgets and turning spits.

● The stables house an exhibition about the Parker family who once owned Saltram and were famous for breeding racehorses.

● The Chapel in the grounds used to be a barn but was adapted by the estate's talented carpenter! It is now an art gallery.

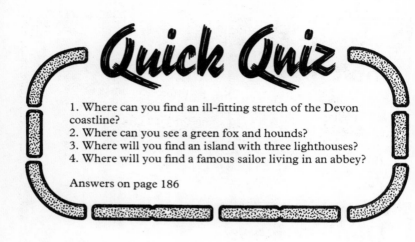

Quick Quiz

1. Where can you find an ill-fitting stretch of the Devon coastline?
2. Where can you see a green fox and hounds?
3. Where will you find an island with three lighthouses?
4. Where will you find a famous sailor living in an abbey?

Answers on page 186

Dorset

Brownsea Island

Poole Harbour BH15 1EE
Tel. Canford Cliffs (0202) 707744
In Poole Harbour. Boats runs from Poole Quay and Sandbanks

When you set foot on Brownsea Island it is as if you are entering a different world. The last private owner of the island, Mr Bonham Christie, is to be thanked for the unspoilt character of the island. She discouraged visitors and gradually let the undergrowth take over, making the island a haven for wildlife.

Canute, landing on Brownsea Island

Don't Miss...

● There are many different habitats on the 500-acre island: seashore, salt marsh, heathland, woodlands, freshwater lakes and a lagoon. This means that there is also a great variety of wildlife: cormorants, curlews and spotted redshank live on the lagoon; red squirrels in the woods and Sika deer on the heathlands.

● You can see the tiny village at the Quay with its row of cottages, church and Customs House which was built to try to stop smuggling.

● If you follow the track to St Andrew's Bay you'll come across the ghost village of Maryland. This was built by Colonel Waugh in the mid-nineteenth century who went bankrupt trying to turn the island into a pottery centre. He built potteries, the village and the church, but the scheme failed and the new buildings were left to decay.

● Family ticket available.

Corfe Castle

Corfe Castle, Wareham
Tel. Corfe Castle (0929) 480921
On A351 Wareham to Swanage road

The ruins straddling the hill above Corfe are all that is left of the magnificent castle built by William the Conqueror in the eleventh century. In those days kings used to travel round the country rather than stay in one palace. Corfe would have been more than just a castle; it was a centre for royal government and administration and a temporary palace.

In 1635 the castle was bought by Sir John Bankes. Only eleven years later the castle was wrecked by Cromwell's men in the Civil War.

Don't Miss...

● Try to imagine what the castle would have looked like in its heyday. You'll be able to see the remains of fireplaces, stairways and garderobes (lavatories).

● Corfe was where Edward the Martyr was poisoned by his stepmother in Anglo-Saxon times. Edward's remains are now in a bank vault in Shaftesbury!

● The castle would have also been used as a prison. There are some grim stories linked to Corfe. One of the nastiest was during the reign of 'bad' King John. At the start of his reign John was challenged by his nephew, Prince Arthur of Brittany. John defeated him at the Battle of Poitou in France and took Arthur and his sister, Eleanor, prisoner. John murdered Arthur and imprisoned Eleanor and 25 Breton knights at Corfe. They tried unsuccessfully to escape and John treated them so badly that 22 of them starved to death.

● Corfe Castle has an excellent defensive site. The castle eventually fell to the Roundheads in the Civil War simply because there was a traitor among its defenders. Sir John's wife, Dame Mary, and her supporters, defended the castle so courageously that the Roundhead general let her keep the keys. After the siege she was always known as 'Brave Dame Mary'.

Essex

Hatfield Forest

Takeley, near Bishop's Stortford
Head Warden: tel. Bishop's Stortford (0279) 870678
3m E of Bishop's Stortford, on S side of A120

Hatfield Forest covers just over 1,000 acres and is one of the last traces of the Royal Forest of Essex which in Norman times

spread over the entire county. It is still criss-crossed with ride
and chases from the time when it was used for royal huntin
parties.

Don't Miss...

● Hatfield Forest is one of the few
large areas of undeveloped land in
Essex and the forest is managed in
traditional fashion with coppicing and
pollarding. For this reason it is a
haven for many animals, birds,
plants and insects once common all
over Essex. It has been named a
Site of Special Scientific Interest.

● The lake in the forest and the shell house
on its banks were created by the Houblon
family who bought the Forest in 1729.

OBSERVATION
HIDE

● You can ride horses in the forest but you
need a permit from the warden. There are
also lakes where you can fish, for which you don't need a permit.

Gloucestershire

Countryside

T he Cotswolds are one of the loveliest areas of Englan
and the Trust protects much of this beautiful part of th
country. Try to visit the following places.

●Dover's Hill, above Weston-sub-Edge – a natural amphi
theatre, and in 1612 the venue for the first 'Cotswold Olimpic
Games'! Captain Robert Dover had the idea of staging th
games with events like wrestling, hammer-throwing and horse
racing accompanied by much feasting and drinking. After

brief ban by Cromwell and his Puritans the games returned under the fun-loving Charles II and continued until the mid-nineteenth century. They have recently had another revival, and if you visit the hill on the Friday after the spring bank holiday you can see this historic event taking place.

Crickley Hill – 5 miles east of Gloucester. There are three trails to follow in this 145-acre country park. Taking the different themes of archaeology, geology and ecology, the trails should help you find out more about the area. There is also a family trail suitable for pushchairs and wheelchairs.

Chedworth Roman Villa

Yanworth, near Cheltenham GL54 3LJ
Tel. Withington (024 289) 256
m NW of Fossebridge on A429

Visit Chedworth Villa and you will get a good idea of the sort of life enjoyed by wealthy landowners in Roman Britain. Chedworth was built in the second century and was at the heart of one of the large farming estates set up by the Romans to provide food and wool for the large town of Cirencester.

Don't Miss...

● There are plans and a children's guide available to lead you around the site.

● The Romans introduced a high standard of hygiene to Britain. The latrine at Chedworth would have had wooden or stone seats over a sewer. Instead of toilet paper, Romans used sponges on sticks which they then washed out in the channel of water running across the floor.

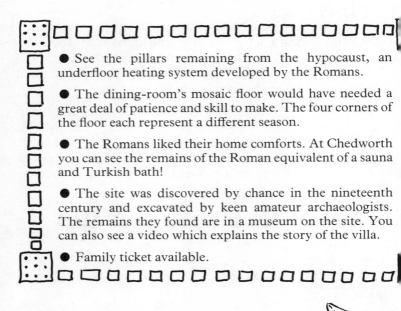

● See the pillars remaining from the hypocaust, an underfloor heating system developed by the Romans.

● The dining-room's mosaic floor would have needed a great deal of patience and skill to make. The four corners of the floor each represent a different season.

● The Romans liked their home comforts. At Chedworth you can see the remains of the Roman equivalent of a sauna and Turkish bath!

● The site was discovered by chance in the nineteenth century and excavated by keen amateur archaeologists. The remains they found are in a museum on the site. You can also see a video which explains the story of the villa.

● Family ticket available.

Snowshill Manor

Near Broadway WR12 7JU
Tel. Broadway (0386) 852410
3m SW of Broadway

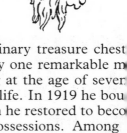

Snowshill Manor is the most extraordinary treasure chest contains over 5,000 objects collected by one remarkable m Charles Wade. Wade started collecting at the age of sever 1890 and this passion continued all his life. In 1919 he bou this Cotswold stone manor house which he restored to beco an enormous show cabinet for his possessions. Among varied treasures are prams, model farm wagons, compas: truncheons, bicycles, musical instruments, glasses and dolls

Don't Miss...

- Wade gave each room in the house a name and his collection was thoughtfully divided amongst them.
- The room called 'Seventh Heaven', which is full of toys.
- The suits of Japanese Samurai armour in the Green Room with their frightening masks.
- Wade didn't live in the manor house (probably because there was no room for him!), but instead lived a very simple life in a little cottage next to the main house.
- Family ticket available.

These names of properties in Gloucestershire have been muddled up. Can you unjumble them?

1. Trodwhech Manor Lilva.
2. Yercklic Lihl.
3. Winsholls Roman.

Answers on page 186

Hampshire

Countryside

The Trust owns three large areas of common land around the edges of the New Forest, where New Forest ponies, cattle and pigs can be seen.

At Bramshaw there are over 1,300 acres of Trust land covering Cadnam and Stocks Cross greens and the commons at

Cadnam, Furzley, Half Moon, Penn and Plaitford. On Furzley Common is a group of Bronze Age round barrows centred on Stagbury Hill. These commons are heavily grazed by cattle and horses and contain important bog areas, heath and woodlands.

● Hale Purlieu and Millersford Plantation are near Fordingbridge. Purlieu means 'land on the border of a forest' and is bound by the laws of the forest controlling the hunting of game. The smaller Hightown Common is near Ringwood.

● The land here is grazed to keep it as open heath, with gorse, heather and some woodland. It is good walking country and even better if you know what to look for.

● The Trust owns 74 acres of meadow and woodland on the banks of the Hamble River. The woodland is managed as nature reserve by the Hampshire and Isle of Wight Naturalist Trust and is open to visitors.

Selbourne Hill

4m S of Alton

The beauty of the parish of Selbourne and the surrounding countryside led its parson, Gilbert White, in 1789 to write book on the area called **The Natural History of Selbourne**. Over two hundred years later the book is still in print. Try to have a look at a copy before you visit and it will help you spot the different flowers, fungi and wildlife of the area.

Remember to consult **The National Trust Handbook** for opening times, admission prices and other details.

Don't Miss...

● Gilbert White's house is now a museum containing some of his possessions and some fascinating objects collected by the Victorian explorers, Frank and Lawrence Oates. The Oates brothers explored southern Africa from 1873 to 1875 and brought back with them examples of life of the bushmen and of native villages. Find out more about the tsetse fly which spreads the mysterious sleeping sickness.

● Lawrence Oates was on Captain Scott's disastrous expedition which tried to reach the South Pole in 1912. You can see photographs of his diary entries, letters and some of the equipment taken on the expedition.

The Vyne

herborne St John, Basingstoke RG26 5DX
el. Basingstoke (0256) 881337
miles N of Basingstoke, between Bramley and Sherborne St John

he Vyne was built between 1500 and 1520 by Sir William andys, who later became Henry VIII's Lord Chamberlain. Henry VIII visited The Vyne three times, and his daughter, lizabeth I, came to the house twice during her reign. In 1653 ie Sandys family sold The Vyne to Chaloner Chute, a ccessful politician, and it stayed in his family until 1956 when ie house was given to the National Trust.

Don't Miss...

● Catherine of Aragon's symbol, the pomegranate, is featured in various places throughout the house. You'll find it carved on the canopies above the stalls in the chapel and in the panelling which lines the walls of the oak gallery.

● Great houses like The Vyne often had a chapel where all of the family, servants and visitors could worship. If you look at the stained-glass windows in The Vyne's chapel, you should be able to find Henry VIII and his first wife, Catherine of Aragon. The window may well have been covered up when Henry VIII made his visit to the house in 1535, as by this date he had divorced Catherine and married Anne Boleyn.

● In the 1770s John Chute built the tomb chamber, off the chapel, in honour of his ancestor, Chaloner Chute. It contains a grand marble monument, which is carved with names of the Chute family and crowned with a life-like, reclining figure of Chaloner Chute.

Hereford and Worcester

Countryside

This is a beautiful part of England and several importan areas of countryside are owned by the Trust, providin good areas for a day out walking. If you want to combin walking, picnicking and have a dose of history, visit Brock hampton Estate. The 1,700-acre estate was given to the Trust i 1946 and there is a network of footpaths and rides to explor through its woods, as well as a landscaped park to picnic in. Tr to visit the half-timbered, moated fourteenth-century man house at Lower Brockhampton and the ruined Norman chap in its grounds.

Berrington Hall

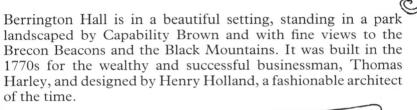

Near Leominster HR6 0DW
Tel. Leominster (0568) 5721
3m N of Leominster on W side of A49

Berrington Hall is in a beautiful setting, standing in a park landscaped by Capability Brown and with fine views to the Brecon Beacons and the Black Mountains. It was built in the 1770s for the wealthy and successful businessman, Thomas Harley, and designed by Henry Holland, a fashionable architect of the time.

Don't Miss...

● The Cawley family bought the estate in 1901 and the Nursery is full of furnishings, pictures and toys from this time. There is a wonderful rocking horse and a miniature four poster bed.

● No expense was spared on the interior decoration and the plasterwork is particularly detailed. Look for the cherubs and seahorses in the drawing room.

● Visit the Victorian laundry and the Georgian tiled dairy in the court at the back of the house.

● Family ticket available.

Croft Castle

Near Leominster HR6 9PW
Tel. Yarpole (056 885) 246
5m NW of Leominster, 9m SW of Ludlow

Croft Castle has belonged to the Croft family almost contin uously since Domesday. Over the years it has gradually been transformed from a medieval fortress into the elegant country house you see today.

Don't Miss...

● Throughout the house you can see paintings of the different members of the Croft family. Some of them are by famous artists, such as the portrait of Elizabeth Cooper, Sir Archer Croft's wife, which was painted by Gainsborough.

● There is a tiny stone church next to the house where many of the Croft family are buried. You can see the early sixteenth-century tomb of Sir Richard Croft and his wife, Dame Eleanor, and get a good idea of what the couple looked like in old age from the effigy.

● Croft Park is famous for its ancient trees. The Spanish chestnut avenue to the west of the castle may well be over 350 years old and some of the oak trees in the park have a girth of more than twenty-five feet!

● If you have time, make sure you follow the footpath from the castle up to the site of the ancient Iron Age hill fort of Croft Ambrey. This was occupied from the fourth century BC until it was abandoned at the Roman Conquest in 50 AD. The view from the fort is spectacular – on a clear day you can see fourteen counties, including much of Wales, from this spot. It is easy to see why it was chosen as a defensive site for a fort.

● Family ticket available.

Hanbury Hall

Droitwich WR9 7EA
Tel. Hanbury (0527 84) 214
4½m E of Droitwich

This attractive red brick country house has hardly been changed since it was built at the beginning of the eighteenth century for the successful barrister, Thomas Vernon. However, most of the contents you'll see in the house are relatively new to Hanbury. The original contents had to be sold in 1790 after the family fortune was lost as a result of the disastrous marriage between Emma Vernon and Henry Cecil.

Don't Miss...

● The house is famous for its Hall and Great Staircase painted by the eighteenth-century mural artist, James Thornhill. The stairway is decorated with mythological scenes and gods, sitting on clouds, look down on you from the ceiling.

● Hanbury once had a splendid formal Dutch-style garden, and a beautifully laid out park. Nothing remains of these now but you can still see the orangery which was built in the middle of the eighteenth century.

● There is an ice house in the grounds. Find out how this was used in the days before refrigerators.

● Family ticket available.

ICE HOUSE

Hertfordshire

Ashridge Estate

Ringshall, Berkhampstead

The Ashridge Estate was originally a monastic property covering over 15,000 acres but was surrendered to the Crown in 153
at the Dissolution of the Monasteries. The estate was sold
1604 to Sir Thomas Egerton and it remained in the family un
1921. The Trust now owns 4,000 acres of open space
commons and woodland of this historic estate.

Don't Miss...

FOOT PATH

● Look out for fallow and muntjac deer, foxes, grey
squirrels and signs of badgers. The estate is also home to
the rare edible dormouse, whose Latin name is *glis glis*.

● Climb to the top of the Ivinghoe Hills at the north end of
the estate and you'll get wonderful views of the surrounding countryside.

● There is a monument on the estate which was erected as
a memorial to the 3rd Duke of Bridgewater one hundred
and fifty years ago. The Duke is described as 'The Father of
Inland Navigation' for his pioneering work in establishing
a canal which connected the family's coal mines in Lancashire to Manchester.

● There is an information centre near the Bridgewater
monument which sells booklets about the estate. There are
many footpaths to help you explore the area.

haw's Corner

ot St Lawrence, near Welwyn AL6 9BX
l. Stevenage (0438) 820307
SW end of Ayot St Lawrence, 2m NE of Wheathampstead

u may have seen the musical **My Fair Lady** but did you
ow it was based on a play called **Pygmalion** by George
rnard Shaw? George Bernard Shaw was a great Irish
aywright with a razor-sharp wit. This was his home from 1906
til his death in 1950 and is where he wrote many of his plays.

Don't Miss...

● The house has hardly been changed since Shaw's death.
His typewriter sits on his desk, with his pens lying beside it
and his dictionaries to hand.

● There is a hut in the garden where Shaw used to go to
write in peace and quiet. After his death his ashes were
scattered in the garden.

● Shaw was a vegetarian. He once said that when he died
'My hearse will be followed not by mourning coaches but
by herds of oxen, sheep, swine, flocks of poultry and a small
travelling aquarium of live fish, all wearing white scarves in
honour of the man who perished rather than eat his fellow
creatures'.

● He was also a health fanatic and a member of the
Cyclist's Touring Club until his death, aged 94.

Isle of Wight

Although the Isle of Wight is small it has a wonderf[...] variety of countryside to explore, much of which [...] owned by the Trust. A few places to visit on the islan[...] are:

● Tennyson Down – 1 mile south east of Freshwater. Name[...] after the poet Alfred, Lord Tennyson, this area of clifftop an[...] downland was one of his favourite places on the island, where [...] used to walk daily. Look out for the two round barrows an[...] signs of prehistoric farming.

● Compton Bay – 1 mile east of Freshwater Bay; the be[...] bathing beach on the Isle of Wight. The coastal walk [...] spectacular and if you are very lucky you may see the ra[...] butterfly, the Granville fritillary, which breeds on the undercli[...]

The Downs – if you walk along the chain of Downs from ottistone to Afton, look out for the downland birdlife – ieatears, larks and pipits. This is a prehistoric ridgeway and u can see groups of Bronze Age barrows.

Visit Mottistone Village where the church and manor house e set around the village green with woodland behind. The anor is not open but you can visit the gardens. You can also go r wonderful walks through the woodland and along the coastal .th on the Mottistone Estate.

Knowles Farm at St Catharine's Point is a wild and beautiful ot at the southerly tip of the island. The area is a particularly od place to birdwatch as migratory birds use it as a stopover . their journeys. Ornithologists have been keeping records of em for many years.

There are footpaths from old Ventnor Station leading up to e highest point on the island at St Boniface Down, above :ntnor.

Borthwood Copse, 2 miles west of Sandown – 60 acres of oodland surviving from the medieval hunting forest which ice covered the eastern part of the island. There are wonderful

bluebells in spring. On the north coast of the island are 14 mil
of tidal creeks, mud flats and salt marshes where you can s
waders and seabirds.

● In the woods near the village of Newtown on the north coa
of the island you may be lucky enough to see red squirrels. Th
is one of their last refuges in England.

● At Bembridge Down you can see the only windmill left on t
island. This four-storey, stone windmill was built around 17
and for the next two hundred years it ground flour, meal a
cattle feed for the surrounding area. It was abandoned in 19
and by 1950 the windmill was derelict. It was partly restor
with money raised locally and came under the care of the Tru
in 1962. You can still see its original machinery and t
enormous 30-foot-long sails.

The Needles Old Battery

West Highdown, Totland Bay PO39 0JH
Tel. Isle of Wight (0983) 754772

The Needles Old Battery was built in 1861 by Lord Palme
ston's government to guard the approaches to the Solent and t
naval base at Portsmouth from possible French invasion. Whe
the Trust acquired the fort, two of the six nineteenth-centu
wrought iron guns lay abandoned below the cliffs. They ha
been thrown over the side in 1903 when new weaponry w
installed. The Trust winched them up from the shore in 198
and one of them has now been remounted on a specially bu
replica gun carriage.

Don't Miss...

● You can reach this magnificently sited fort by walking from Alum Bay up to the Needles headland.

● The powder magazine contains an exhibition of the history of the Needles headland.

● Make sure you see the chambers which were used for storing gunpowder, shells and cartridges.

● There is a 200-foot-long tunnel from the parade ground to the lookout point at the tip of the headland. You can get a good view of the Needles, sea stacks which have been separated from the headland through erosion by the sea. The tallest pinnacle, named Lot's Wife after the character in the Bible who was turned into a pillar of salt, collapsed in 1764, but three pinnacles still exist.

Kent

Countryside

At Pegwell Bay there are hundreds of acres of saltings, sand dunes and mudflats rich in bird life. If you are interested in birds this is a wonderful place to visit as there is a hide from which you can watch the migrant waders, British sea and shore birds and some rare species which come to the area. There are also lots of footpaths to explore.

● At Langdon Cliffs look out for the only breeding colony of kittiwakes in Kent. This area of chalk grassland is rich in wild flowers and on a clear day you can see France from the cliffs. From here you can walk along the white cliffs to South Foreland Lighthouse.

● The Kent countryside was badly hit by the storm of 1987. However, after a lot of hard work, many of the gardens and areas of countryside are recovering and again looking beautiful, if different.

Chartwell

Westerham TN16 1PS
Tel. Edenbridge (0732) 866368
2m S of Westerham off B2026

Chartwell is a house full of the spirit of its last owner, the great politician Sir Winston Churchill, who lived here from 1922 until just before his death in 1965. It was very much a family home and all the rooms in the house are just as they were when the Churchills lived here.

Don't Miss...

● If you're interested in the history of the Second World War there should be plenty to interest you at Chartwell. Just look in the visitors' book and you'll see some of the great names of the era who stayed at Chartwell. There is also an exhibition on Churchill's role as war-time Prime Minister.

● You might bump into Jock, the Chartwell cat. Churchill owned a cat called Jock and requested that there should always be a Jock at Chartwell to have free run of the house. The first Jock is buried in the garden, along with Churchill's favourite poodles – their graves are marked by small headstones.

● Find the summerhouse which Churchill built for his children in the garden.

Ightham Mote

Ivy Hatch, Sevenoaks TN15 0NT
Tel. Plaxtol (0732) 810378
6m E of Sevenoaks, off A25, and 2½m S of Ightham, off A227

Ightham Mote is a beautiful and rare example of a medieval moated manor house. It has been extended and modernised since the original house was built in the 1340s but has kept its romantic charm.

Don't Miss...

● The trip through the house leads you on a journey through time. The house was begun in the Middle Ages, but changes were made up until 1900 with additions like the Billiard Room.

● In 1521 the house was bought by a courtier, Richard Clement. He was responsible for much of the heraldic and armorial decoration around the house, which often reflects his loyalty to the Tudors. The window in the Great Hall carries the Tudor Rose together with the pomegranate, the symbol of Henry VIII's first wife, Catherine of Aragon. Only a few years later this window became out of date when Henry abandoned Catherine for Anne Boleyn.

● Stroll round the gardens and watch the enormous golden orfe fish swimming in the moat.

● When Sir Thomas and Lady Colyer-Fergusson brought their dog, Dido, to Ightham Mote in 1891 they built her a very special kennel – a mini-version of the main house! It still stands in the courtyard.

● In 1872 alterations were made to the Great Hall to make it more habitable. A small cupboard doorway which had been blocked up was opened to reveal a skeleton of a woman. Nobody knows who she was or how she got there.

Quick Quiz

1. Where in Kent can you find a luxury dog kennel?
2. At which Kent property will you always be able to find a Scottish sounding cat?
3. Where can you find a fort which sounds like something out of a sewing basket?

Answers on page 186

Lancashire

Rufford Old Hall

Rufford, near Ormskirk LA40 1SG
Tel. Rufford (0704) 821254
m N of Ormskirk

Rufford Old Hall was built by Sir Thomas Hesketh *c*.1420 and was one of the finest buildings in the county. Only the Great Hall survives from the original house.

Don't Miss...

● The Great Hall is 46 feet long and 22 feet wide and has a wonderful timber-framed ceiling decorated with the coats of arms of great Lancastrian families. Some say that William Shakespeare acted in this hall.

● All around the house are weapons and armour dating back to the sixteenth century. You'll see from the size of some of the suits of armour that as a rule people are taller nowadays.

● Make sure you visit the Philip Ashcroft Museum of Rural Life in the outbuildings. There are displays of what life would have been like for villagers before the industrial revolution. This is the place to go if you've never seen a man-trap!

● There is a sad ghost story connected to Rufford Old Hall. During the Middle Ages the Ashurst Beacon used to be lit to summon the men of Lancashire to fight off invasions by the Scots. At the engagement party of Elizabeth Hesketh, the daughter of the house, the beacon was lit. Her fiancé left the party to fight the Scots and was killed. Elizabeth refused to believe he was dead and insisted that the preparations for the wedding continue. Her ghost is said to haunt the house waiting for her fiancé to return.

Lincolnshire

Belton House

Grantham NG32 2LS
Tel. Grantham (0476) 66116
3m NE of Grantham on A607

WILLIAM of ORANGE

William III was entertained at Belton in 1695, ten years after th house was built for Sir John Brownlow. Twelve oxen and sixt sheep were killed for the royal feast and the king fed so well tha when he got to his next stop, Lincoln, he 'could eat nothing but mess of milk'. It wasn't only the food which William would hav found rich – the house is filled with fine carvings and plaster work, luxurious furniture and valuable paintings and tapestrie

Don't Miss...

● The painted floor in the Tyrconnel Room showing the Brownlow coat of arms. Greyhounds were part of the family crest and you'll see them in various other forms around the house.

● The tapestries in the Tapestry Room are very rare. They were found being used as carpets in the attic at the end of the last century and were rescued by the 3rd Earl Brownlow.

● The 6th Earl Brownlow was Lord in Waiting to Edward VIII during his short reign. Edward often stayed at Belton and there is a display of newspaper cuttings and items in the Flower Room which tell the story leading to the king's abdication in 1936.

● The garden is full of fascinating sculpture and buildings. The book *Moondial* (later a television series) by Helen Cresswell was inspired by the sundial clasped by Father Time.

● There is an adventure playground and in summer there are boat and miniature train rides in the park.

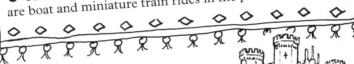

Tattershall Castle

Tattershall, Lincoln LN4 4LR
Tel. Coningsby (0526) 42543
½m SE of Woodhall Spa on S side of A153

The first castle on this site was built by Robert Tateshale in 1231. Nearly two hundred years later Ralph, Lord Cromwell inherited Tattershall from his grandmother. Cromwell was an

extraordinary man: he had fought in the battle of Agincourt, ~~at~~
the age of 12! He was a very influential man and was Treasurer
of England among other responsibilities. He was also extremely
rich and used some of his money to build the tower we see today.

Don't Miss...

- Cromwell made sure that his new home reflected his wealth. There are grand spiral staircases, magnificent fireplaces, vaulted corridors and traceried windows.

- You will see Cromwell's badge, the Treasurer's purse, carved in many places around the tower.

- On a clear day you can see Lincoln cathedral from the roof.

- There is a museum in the guardhouse with a model of what the castle would have looked like in its heyday.

Woolsthorpe Manor

Woolsthorpe, Colsterworth, Nr Grantham
Tel. Grantham (0476) 860338
7m S of Grantham, ½m NW of Colsterworth, 1m W of A1

A Christmas Day genius was born at Woolsthorpe in 1642. He
was Isaac Newton, the great scientist. Many of his discoveries
were made at Woolsthorpe Manor where he lived with his
grandmother.

Don't Miss...

● When Newton was nine, he made an accurate sundial and measured the strength of storms by comparing jumps he made on windy days with those he made on calm days.

● In 1661 he went to study at Cambridge, but returned to Woolsthorpe when the University was closed by the Plague in 1665. That year he discovered the principle of differential calculus. In later years he worked out the theory of gravity and showed that sunlight was not white, but made up of a mixture of specific colours, the spectrum.

● You can visit the simple room where Newton worked. It is now hung with prints of other famous seventeenth-century scientists.

● Find the upright desk which Newton may have worked at. In the seventeenth century it was fashionable to write while standing up.

London

Ham House

Ham, Richmond TW10 7RS
Tel. 081-940 1950 (code before May 1990 is 01)
On S bank of Thames, W of A307, at Petersham

The best way to approach Ham House is to take the ferry across the Thames from Twickenham and walk up through the grounds to the house.

Elizabeth, Countess of Dysart, wasn't satisfied with inheriting her father's Jacobean house – she wanted something better.

When her first husband died she married her close friend, the Earl of Lauderdale, in 1672, and together they set about enlarging and improving the house. This haughty couple produced one of the most lavish and extravagant houses of the day.

Don't Miss...

● The house is presented as it would have looked in the seventeenth century when the Lauderdales lived there. Fortunately many of the inventories have survived and these were used to make the house appear as authentic as possible.

● Make sure you see the kitchen in the basement. You can see the sort of utensils and food used in those days and get some idea of what life would have been like for the Lauderdales' cook and the scullions 300 years ago.

● The garden has been planted as it might have been in the seventeenth century. A formal layout for the lawn leads to a network of paths through the 'wilderness' of hornbeam hedges. You can also see a typical seventeenth-century knot garden.

Osterley Park

Isleworth, Middlesex TW7 4RB
Tel. 081-560 3918 (before May 1990 the code is 01)
N of Osterley station with access from Syon Lane, N side of Great West Road A4

Osterley Park was originally built for Queen Elizabeth I's Chancellor of the Exchequer, Sir Thomas Gresham. It was transformed in the eighteenth century into a grand, Neo-classical palace by the famous Scottish architect, Robert Adam. The land outside Osterley's 140-acre park has been heavily built up and is now part of London's suburbs, but when you drive through Osterley's gates it's as though you're entering a country estate.

Don't Miss...

● There are some wonderful places to explore in the park: the semi-circular greenhouse designed by Adam, the garden temple and the long winding lake.

● There is a park leaflet describing the different species of trees and plants to look for in the park. Keep your eyes open for the rabbits and squirrels.

● Some of the oak trees are about 400 years old and were planted by the original owner, Sir Thomas Gresham.

● The Elizabethan stables have been converted into tea-rooms but you can still see the stalls for the horses.

● As well as the grand state rooms in the house, you can see the servants' quarters and imagine what life 'below stairs' was like.

Merseyside

Speke Hall

The Walk, Liverpool L24 1XD
Tel. 051-427 7231
On N bank of Mersey, 8m SE of centre of Liverpool, 1m S of A561

Speke Hall is a beautiful, half-timbered, moated Elizabethan manor house which was built from 1490 by three successive generations of the Norris family.

Don't Miss...

● The best way to approach Speke is to walk over the Elizabethan stone bridge which used to cross the moat, go through the massive studded wooden doors and into the courtyard where two yew trees – Adam and Eve – guard the house.

● The Norris family were Catholics and there are many hiding places in the house which would have sheltered priests or fleeing Catholics. There is also a spy hole in one of the bedrooms.

● Visit the kitchen and servants' hall to get an idea of what life 'below stairs' at Speke was like.

● It is said that the Tapestry Room is visited by a ghost who walks across the room and disappears into the wall. When this part of the wall was examined, a secret passageway was found.

● Family ticket available.

Norfolk

Countryside

The Trust owns some important areas of the North Norfolk coast. If you're interested in bird and wildlife you should try to visit Blakeney Point, a 3½-mile long [sa]nd and shingle spit. In the summer you can see terns, [oy]stercatchers and many other kinds of seabirds. There is also a [la]rge grey seal colony, so you should be able to see basking seals.

The rolling parkland of Sheringham Park is the work of one of [En]gland's greatest landscape designers, Humphry Repton. The [pa]rkland has good views of the sea and its woodlands contain [m]any different varieties of rhododendrons and azaleas. The [lan]d slopes gently down to the cliffs which are slowly being [wo]rn away due to the effects of the sea and wind. This stretch of [co]astline has been noted as a Site of Special Scientific Interest [fo]r its geological formation and its birds nesting along the cliff-[fac]e.

Blickling Hall

[Bl]ickling, Norwich NR11 6NF
[Te]l. Aylsham (0263) 733084
[O]n N side of B1354, 1½m NW of Aylsham

[T]here has been a manor house at Blickling for hundreds of [ye]ars. The present building dates from 1620 and was built for [Si]r Henry Hobart. It is set in parkland and even has a lake of its [ow]n.

Don't Miss...

● The bull was the crest of the Hobart family and there are Hobart bulls all over the house, made of wood, plaster and stone.

● Henry VIII's second wife, Anne Boleyn, spent her childhood at Blickling. It is said that on the anniversary of her execution she can be seen riding up to the house in a coach pulled by headless horses, driven by a headless coachman and holding her head in her lap!

● The 123-foot Long Gallery with its elaborate plaster ceiling. The walls are covered in books, many of which are very rare.

● The basement kitchen is full of old kitchen equipment for you to see the sort of conditions in which servants worked.

● Take time to explore the gardens and park and find the temple, orangery and secret garden with its summerhouse and sundial.

● Blickling has a secret room in the roof (not open) – the Punishment Room – where rude servants were locked up to improve their manners. Its walls are covered in graffiti.

● The Hawk Trust has an interesting exhibition in Blickling village hall about barn owls, showing the dangers threatening these birds.

Felbrigg Hall

orwich NR11 8PR
el. West Runton (026 375) 444
ear Felbrigg village, 2m SW of Cromer off A148

elbrigg was the home of the Windham family for over three
undred years. The estate was bought for the family in 1459 and
1620 Thomas Windham started building the hall. A wing was
lded in 1686 by his son and the house has hardly been altered
nce.

Don't Miss...

● Many Victorians used to shoot and stuff birds to form
their private collections. Thomas Wyndham Cremer was
one such man and when he died in 1894 he had collected
160 different species of birds. They now provide a valuable
record of the birdlife around Felbrigg in the nineteenth
century.

● Birds also feature in the ornate plasterwork in the west
wing where the plasterer modelled pheasants, woodcock,
partridges and plover.

● Another member of the family, William Windham, was
fascinated by boats. He had one on the lake in the park and
his fascination can still be seen in the many seascapes
hanging on the walls in the house.

● In the walled garden is an octagonal
dovecote topped by a weathervane in
the shape of a peacock. Doves still live
there and are fed by the gardeners.

● There are acres of parkland
and woods to explore.

Oxburgh Hall

Oxborough, near King's Lynn PE33 9PS
Tel. Gooderstone (036621) 258
At Oxborough, 7m SW of Swaffham on S side of Stoke Ferry road

Can you believe that Oxburgh Hall, today surrounded by field
used to stand on an island in the middle of a marsh? The marsh
have now been drained and put to agricultural use. The Hall ha
also changed since it was built as a manor house in the elevent
century.

Don't Miss...

Mary Queen of Scots making her embroidery seem less tedious.

● The panels of
needlework made
by Mary Queen of
Scots while she was
a prisoner in the
custody of the Earl of
Shrewsbury on the order of
her cousin, Elizabeth I. She
copied pictures of birds,
animals, fish and insects
from illustrations in a
sixteenth-century book of
natural history and used many
different colours to 'make the
worke seem lesse tedious'.

● The Bedingfeld family who came to Oxburgh in the sixteenth century were devout Catholics. There is a priest's hole in the gatehouse, a reminder of the days when the family would have had to practise their religion in secret.

● The collection of Civil War weapons and armour in the gatehouse.

Northamptonshire

Canons Ashby House

Canons Ashby, Daventry NN11 6SD
Tel. Blakesley (0327) 860044
On B4525 Northampton to Banbury Road

This ancient courtyard house needed an enormous amount of restoration work when it came to the Trust in 1981. Dry rot, collapsing ceilings and death-watch beetle all threatened its survival. The house takes its name from the Augustinian Priory which once dominated the prosperous medieval village. All that is left of the village are bumps and furrows, but part of the grand priory church is still standing.

Don't Miss...

● The domed ceiling in the Drawing Room with its strange plaster ceiling decorated with thistles, pomegranates and heads of Indian princesses!

● The terraced gardens. The third layer is planted with species of apples and pears that were known in sixteenth-century England. The bottom terrace is a wild garden full of meadow flowers.

● There is a 70-acre park to explore.

Northumberland

Northumberland has a beautiful stretch of coastline, with castles, sandy beaches, nature reseves and rocky offshor islands. There are also fascinating places to explor inland.

Here are a few ideas of places to visit.

● From Craster to Low Newton there is a 2½-mile walk along th sand dunes. Visit the nature reserve at Newton Pool and carr on walking to the spectacular ruins of the fourteenth-centur Dunstanburgh Castle.

● Just south of Craster at Howick are 189 acres of cliffs and san dunes. The geological formation of the cliffs and the nesting fulmars have made this a Site of Special Scientific Interest Footpaths at Low Stead Farm lead down to the sandy beach.

● Ross Castle, 12 miles north west of Alnwick, is the remains c an Iron Age hill fort. It's worth climbing the hill for the views t Holy Island, Bamburgh Castle and the Farne Islands.

St Cuthbert's Cave, 10 miles north east of Wooler, is a natural one cave set in the Kyloe Hills. It is said to have been one of the sting places for the body of the early English missionary, St uthbert, on its journey from Holy Island to Durham Cathedral the seventh century.

Lady's Well at Holystone, 7 miles west of Rothbury, is a eaceful natural spring in a grove of fir trees. Early in the venth century the English bishop, Paulinus, baptised about ,000 people here. It is also said to be the place where St Ninian ad baptised thousands of converts in the fifth century.

There are over 200 acres of woodland to explore at Allen nks, 3 miles west of Haydon Bridge. The trees were planted the eighteenth and nineteenth centuries as the pleasure ounds of Ridley Hall. There are now over 14 miles of otpaths. Look out for roe deer and red squirrels.

Cragside

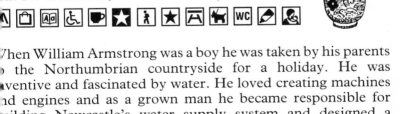

othbury, Morpeth NE65 7PX
el. Rothbury (0669) 20333
m SW of Alnwick, 1m N of Rothbury

hen William Armstrong was a boy he was taken by his parents the Northumbrian countryside for a holiday. He was ventive and fascinated by water. He loved creating machines d engines and as a grown man he became responsible for uilding Newcastle's water supply system and designed a ater-powered crane.

In 1863 he decided to build a house overlooking the stream here he had spent many happy holidays as a boy. Cragside was house with a difference...

Don't Miss...

● Armstrong harnessed the water on the estate to power all sorts of contraptions in the house: a lift, a rotating roasting spit in the kitchen, plant pots to turn to the sun in the greenhouse plus many other machines on the property.

● By 1880 Cragside was the first house in the world to be lit by hydro-electric power.

● Armstrong planted millions of trees on the bare hillsides of the 1,725 acres surrounding Cragside and created pleasure grounds with 40 miles of carriage drives and walks which you can explore.

● A circular walk called the Power Circuit takes you around the main hydraulic and hydro-electric machinery on the estate.

● The old stable block has been turned into the Armstrong Energy Centre where you can find out about the production, use and conservation of energy.

Farne Islands

–5m off Northumberland coast, opposite Bamburgh. Boats from Seahouses Harbour

The Farne Islands were given to the Trust in 1925 and are a very important nature reserve and bird sanctuary. The sea has a good supply of fish and this makes the islands a popular summer home and breeding ground for over 50,000 pairs of birds. Other birds stay all the year round, some visit in winter and migrating birds use the islands as a stopover on their long flights.

Don't Miss...

● There are boat trips from Seahouses Harbour to the islands every day, weather permitting.

● Seventeen different species of seabird use the islands including puffins, guillemots, kittiwakes, eider duck, fulmar and Arctic tern.

● Atlantic seals have been recorded on the islands for over 800 years. Fortunately the seals here were only slightly affected by the deadly virus in 1988.

● The Farnes also have a religious association going back hundreds of years. Monks lived on the Inner Farne for over eight centuries and St Cuthbert died here in 687.

Hadrian's Wall and Housesteads Fort

Bardon Mill, Hexham NE47 6NN
Custodian: tel. Bardon Mill (049 84) 363
6m NE of Haltwhistle, 4m N of Bardon Mill railway station

Eighty years after their conquest of Britain the Romans were
still finding it hard to control the fierce northern tribes of the
Picts and Scots. When the Emperor Hadrian visited Britain in
AD 122 he ordered the construction of a wall to stretch right
across the country from Newcastle to Carlisle to mark the
northernmost limit of the Roman Empire and to keep out the
barbarians. The wall was carefully planned with thirteen main

110

rts along its length, interspersed with smaller milecastles and
atch towers. The Trust owns a stretch of wall from House-
teads to Steel Rigg, including the remains of Housesteads Fort.

Don't Miss...

● The pillars which used to support the wooden floor of the granary, letting air circulate to keep the grain dry.

● The latrine system which had enough seats for thirty soldiers!

● A museum with archaeological finds from the excavations of the area. There are also plans and models to help you imagine what the fort looked like in its heyday.

● You can walk along the wall and think what it was like for the Roman soldiers serving here, including men from North Africa and Italy who must have found this part of the country very cold.

Wallington

ambo, Morpeth NE61 4AR
el. Scots' Gap (067 074) 283
m W of Morpeth off B6343

ir John Fenwick of Wallington was beheaded in 1697 for
otting to assassinate William III. Fenwick got his own back...
ter his death! He bred horses and his favourite, White Sorrell,
as confiscated by the king. However, William had a fatal riding

accident in Hampton Court Park when White Sorrell tripped o[n]
a molehill and threw the king. From then onwards the mo[le]
became the toast of the Stuart supporters, the Jacobites, wh[o]
would raise their glasses to 'the little gentleman in black velvet'

Don't Miss...

● Maria Wilson, the wife of the 5th Baronet, Sir John Trevelyan, came to Wallington in 1791. She was a great collector of porcelain – you can see an odd tea set in the parlour which has life-size insects painted on the bottom of each cup. She also set up the Cabinet of Curiosities which is full of strange objects from a piece of Edward IV's coffin to a stuffed porcupine fish.

● The huge paintings in the Great Hall of incidents in Northumbrian history. The artistic Lady Pauline Trevelyan commissioned William Bell Scott to paint these and she and her pre-Raphaelite friends helped to paint the dividing flower panels.

● The collection of dolls' houses in the Servants' Hall. These date from 1835 to 1930 and range from the enormous Hammond House which is over 8ft tall to the Mouse House which can only be seen through two keyholes and a mouse hole.

● There is lots to see in the grounds: a Jacobean walled garden, a wonderful conservatory and four huge stone griffin heads on the lawn.

● You can walk in the woods near the house or try one of two waymarked walks across the estate making use of two disused railway lines.

Nottinghamshire

Clumber Park

The Estate Office
Clumber Park, Worksop S80 3AZ
Tel. Worksop (0909) 476592
½m SE of Worksop

Clumber Park's 3,800 acres of heath, grassland, farmland and woodland used to surround the country house of the Dukes of Newcastle. The house was demolished in 1938, but the stable block and chapel were saved along with the park and its garden buildings.

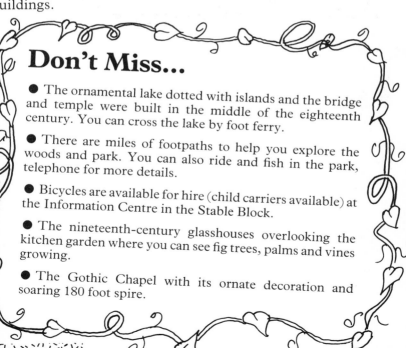

Don't Miss...

● The ornamental lake dotted with islands and the bridge and temple were built in the middle of the eighteenth century. You can cross the lake by foot ferry.

● There are miles of footpaths to help you explore the woods and park. You can also ride and fish in the park, telephone for more details.

● Bicycles are available for hire (child carriers available) at the Information Centre in the Stable Block.

● The nineteenth-century glasshouses overlooking the kitchen garden where you can see fig trees, palms and vines growing.

● The Gothic Chapel with its ornate decoration and soaring 180 foot spire.

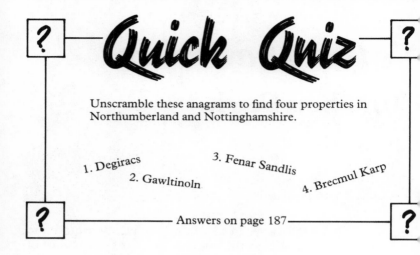

Answers on page 187

Oxfordshire

Countryside

The Trust protects about 10,000 acres of farmland, woods and hills of Oxfordshire's rolling countryside.

● White Horse Hill, Uffington, 6 miles west of Wantage. Set 800 feet up in the Berkshire Downs this 320-foot long White Horse was probably carved out of the chalk during the Iron Age and may have marked the territory of a local tribe. At the foot of the hill is the Manger, a sheltered grassy area where it is said the horse comes to feed!

● The hill is crowned by the Iron Age hill fort of Uffington Castle, which dates from the first century BC. The ancient route, the Ridgeway, crosses the crest of the Downs.

● Nearby is Dragons Hill, traditionally the site where St George slew the dragon. There is a bare patch of earth where it is said the dragon's blood was spilt and nothing will grow.

All three monuments are owned by the National Trust but are looked after by English Heritage.

Try to visit Great Coxwell Barn, near Faringdon. This is an enormous, 152-foot-long tithe barn which belonged to the Cistercian abbey of Beaulieu and was built in the middle of the thirteenth century. In the Middle Ages people were expected to give one tenth (tithe) of their crops to the church as a tax. Enormous barns like this one were built in order to hold all the grain. These buildings are very popular with barn owls which can hunt the mice and rats eating the grain.

Greys Court

Rotherfield Greys, Henley-on-Thames RG9 4PG
Tel. Rotherfield Greys (049 17) 529
5m W of Henley-on-Thames on A423

In the seventeenth century Greys Court became a 'prison' for two of the famous figures of the day. In 1613 James I's favourite, Robert Carr, and his wife Frances were found guilty of the murder of the poet Sir Thomas Overbury who was found poisoned in the Tower of London. James could not escape punishing them in some way and so chose to banish them to live at Greys Court, the home of Frances's sister. If you visit, you'll see it can't have been a great hardship for Carr and his wife.

Don't Miss...

● The donkey wheel which dates back to Tudor times. The large wheel is mounted over a well cut 200 foot into the chalk. As the donkey paced the boards of the wheel, it powered large buckets of water to be hoisted from the well and into a tank in the roof.

● The Archbishop's Maze, opened in 1981 by Dr Robert Runcie.

● The ruins of the fourteenth-century manor house can still be seen, although most are now overgrown with plants from the gardens.

You may have found your way out of the Archbishop's Maze at Greys Court but can you get out of this one?

Answers on page 186

Shropshire

Attingham Park

Shrewsbury SY4 4TP
Tel. Upton Magna (074377) 203
4m SE of Shrewsbury

No dogs in deer park

Noel Hill, 1st Lord Berwick, poured his fortune into building this magnificent eighteenth-century house. Set in beautiful parkland, Attingham is an imposing house with eighty rooms, many of which are filled with valuable furniture and art collected by the 1st Lord Berwick and his descendants.

Don't Miss...

● You'll see superb English and Italian furniture, paintings and textiles as you wander round the house. Don't be put off by the rope barriers, blinds on the windows and notices saying 'don't touch'. These measures have to be taken so that the house and contents are protected for future generations.

● Attingham's Picture Gallery was designed in 1805 to house the 2nd Lord Berwick's collection of pictures which he had bought on his travels abroad. Unfortunately the roof leaked, and a large sum of money had to be spent on roof repairs only a couple of years later.

● There used to be an extremely well stocked cellar in the vaults. There are records from the 1808 cellar book itemising four hundred bottles of sherry, three hundred bottles of port and hundreds of bottles of other spirits and wines. The vaults now contain a magnificent collection of silver, including an entire silver dinner service.

117

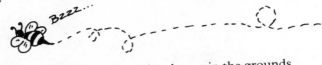

● There is a dainty white bee house in the grounds.

● Take time to explore the park. Much of the tree planting was planned by the famous landscape architect, Humphry Repton in the late eighteenth century. A large herd of fallow deer grazes in the deer park.

Wenlock Edge

E of A49 near Much Wenlock

Can you imagine that Wenlock Edge used to be a barrier reef! 420 million years ago a deep ocean covered the land to the west and the limestone of this area is built up mainly from the skeletons of sea creatures.

Don't Miss...

● During the Civil War, Thomas Smallman, the owner of nearby Wilderhope Manor and a Royalist, was imprisoned in his home by the Roundheads. He managed to escape and avoided capture by riding his horse over Wenlock Edge. Smallman's horse was killed but his own fall was broken by a tree. This spot is now known as Major's Leap.

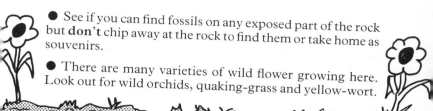

- See if you can find fossils on any exposed part of the rock but **don't** chip away at the rock to find them or take home as souvenirs.

- There are many varieties of wild flower growing here. Look out for wild orchids, quaking-grass and yellow-wort.

Somerset

Countryside

Somerset has a glorious mixture of countryside to explore: beautiful coastline, hills, moorland, wooded valleys and rich farmland.

●The Holnicote Estate contains 20 square miles of some of England's most beautiful countryside and wonderful walking country. Horner Wood contains 900 acres of oak forest dating back to the Iron Age, and is probably the largest area of ancient woodland in England. It's also famous as a habitat for lichens. If you're walking on the estate's moorland look out for buzzards soaring in the sky and wild red deer.

●There are walks with good views at Beacon and Bicknoller hills, west of Williton and an Iron Age hill fort to see at Trendle Ring.

●Ebbor Gorge, near Wells, is a wooded, steep-sided limestone valley rich in history and wildlife. The only way it can be seen is by foot and there are a selection of nature walks to help you do this. Look out for signs of badgers living in the woods, and you may also be lucky enough to see buzzards and sparrowhawks wheeling around. There are caves and rock shelters which were lived in from the early Stone Age but are now just home to horseshoe bats.

● A steep path with steps cut into the hillside leads to the top of Brean Down at Weston Bay. This peninsula has many reminders that man has lived here for thousands of years: there are barrows, burial cairns, an Iron Age fort, the foundations of a Roman temple and Celtic field systems. You can also see the ruins of a nineteenth-century fort which was built to defend the mainland from French attackers sailing up the Bristol Channel. There is a bird sanctuary here and good fishing from the rocks.

Dunster Castle

Dunster, near Minehead TA24 6SL
Tel. Dunster (0643) 821314
In Dunster, 3m SE of Minhead on A396

*In village – not NT

The site at Dunster has been fortified for hundreds of years. None of the original defences survives and the fantasy castle with its turrets, battlements and towers was mostly created in the nineteenth century for the owner, George Luttrell.

Cromwell besieging Dunster Castle

Don't Miss...

● An exhibition in the Tenants Hall shows how the present-day castle evolved from the original Norman fortifications.

● The staircase carved with cherubs and different hunting scenes and the three-dimensional plaster ceiling in the Dining Room along the same theme.

● The magnificent seventeenth-century stables which survived the Civil War. Before the Second World War polo tournaments were held every year at Dunster and the stables were filled to capacity. They are still used occasionally.

● The priest's hole hidden off the King's Bedroom. Some say a passage used to connect it to the stables at the bottom of the hill.

● The pets' cemetery.

● The reservoir, a 40,000 gallon chamber just below the keep, which used to supply the castle and the village.

Montacute House

ntacute TA15 6XP
. Martock (0935) 823289
Montacute village, 4m W of Yeovil, on S side of A3088

ntacute was built for the successful lawyer Sir Edward lips at the end of the sixteenth century. Because it was built time of peace and prosperity the house is unfortified and the

builder could spend more attention on its decoration
external appearance, so Montacute has lovely stone carvi
and huge windows. The stone came from the local H
quarries.

Don't Miss...

● The 'nine worthies' on the east front of the house: three
worthies, or heroes, come from the Old Testament, three
from classical mythology, and three from British history.
They all wear Roman costume and indicate that Lawyer
Phelips knew about the fashionable Continental style of
decorating a building with classical statues.

● There are some detailed needlework hangings in the
house which show the fashion of Dutch gardens at the time
of William and Mary, neatly laid out with orange trees in
tubs put out for the summer.

● The National Portrait Gallery has loaned the Trust a
collection of Elizabethan and Jacobean portraits to hang in
the Long Gallery. You can see pictures of some of the most
famous people of the time: Walter Raleigh, Francis Drake
and Lord Burleigh, Elizabeth's Chancellor.

● The garden is based on an Elizabethan design. There are
raised walks, garden pavilions, and an orangery to explore.

Remember to consult **The National Trust
Handbook** for opening times, admission
prices and other details.

Staffordshire

Moseley Old Hall

seley Old Hall Lane,
dhouses, Wolverhampton WV10 7HY
. Wolverhampton (0902) 782808
N of Wolverhampton, S of M54 between A449 and A460

is Elizabethan house has played a significant part in this
ntry's history. The house has a secret room where many
tholic priests hid during times of persecution and which
ed the life of King Charles II during the Civil War. In
tember 1651 the Royalists were
eated by Cromwell's army at the
ttle of Worcester. Charles escaped,
guised himself as a woodcutter
d arrived in the dead of night at
seley Old Hall. When the
undheads came to search the
use he was hidden in a
all space built between two
drooms, with an entrance through
rapdoor in a cupboard leading to an
ape route up the chimney! Charles
s not found and later escaped to
ance.

Don't Miss...

● You can retrace Charles' route on that fateful night almost three hundred and fifty years ago. The house has changed little since that time.

● There are portraits of Charles and of those people who helped him to escape. You can also see a proclamation offering a £1,000 reward for the capture of the king and a letter of thanks from Charles II to Jane Lane who helped him escape.

● A small garden has been created using only plants which were grown in the seventeenth century. There is a knot garden, an orchard planted with old varieties of fruit tree and a small herb garden.

● Family ticket available.

Shugborough

Milford, near Stafford ST17 0XB
Tel. Little Haywood (0889) 881388
6m E of Stafford on A513, entrance to Milford

Shugborough has been the home of the Anson family since 16 when William Anson purchased the estate. His two sor Thomas and George, are responsible for how the house a estate look today. George went to sea at the age of twelve a became a famous and wealthy Admiral. He used his money help his cultivated brother, Thomas, enlarge and improve t family estate using top-class architects, landscape designe craftsmen and decorators.

Don't Miss...

● Thomas was a great admirer of the arts of classical Greece and the interior of the house was decorated to this taste with columns, classical statues and busts.

● Thomas also had a good collection of paintings. Many of these had to be sold in 1842 to pay off the debts of the 2nd Viscount though, luckily, some were kept. Thomas was also keen on farming and had a herd of rare Corsican goats; he even went as far as having their portraits painted. You can see these in the Drawing Room.

● There is a monument in the grounds dedicated to Admiral Anson's cat who travelled with his master on his four-year voyage round the world.

● Shugborough Park Farm was built as the estate farm in 1805. It is now a working farm museum and a centre for rare breeds of farm animals. You can see shire horses, Tamworth pigs, Bagot goats, long horn cattle and many other types of animal.

● There are demonstrations of traditional methods of farming and you can see the type of tools and machinery used in the nineteenth century.

● Make sure you see the working flour mill on the farm. You can also see demonstrations of cheese- and butter-making in the dairy.

- The Staffordshire County Museum is housed in the stables and outbuildings and will give you an idea of what life was like in the nineteenth century. Here you can see reconstructions of a land agent's office, a nineteenth-century schoolroom, an Edwardian nursery as well as displays on medicine and crime and punishment. The kitchens, laundry and brew house have all been restored to working order and demonstrations are given so you can see how the servants worked.

- There are many events planned at Shugborough during the holidays. Telephone to find out what's going on.

- Family ticket available.

Suffolk

Ickworth

The Rotunda, Horringer, Bury St Edmunds
Tel. Horringer (028 488) 270
In Horringer, 3m SW of Bury St Edmunds on W side of A143

This strangely shaped house was built for Frederick August Hervey, the eccentric 4th Earl of Bristol and Bishop of Derr Hervey had a large income and inherited a fortune which spent on travelling abroad and collecting works of art which planned to display at Ickworth. Unfortunately he never saw t house completed as he died in 1803 on one of his trips to Ita His body was shipped back to England labelled as an 'antiq statue'!

Don't Miss...

● The estate has been owned by the Herveys since the middle of the fifteenth century and the house is full of porcelain, paintings, furniture and silver which the family has collected over the years. There is an entire cabinet filled with silver objects in the shape of fish.

SWORDFISH

● There is a taped guide which takes you on a tour of the house with stories about the eccentric Earl Bishop and memories of Lady Phyllis MacRae who lived at Ickworth before the Second World War.

● Explore the gardens and the 800-acre park. Find the old walled garden, summer house and terrace walk. The Silver Garden has a mass of bluebells in spring growing around hexagonal basalt stones brought back from the Giant's Causeway in Ireland. There are deer in the park and woodland walks.

Remember to consult **The National Trust Handbook** for opening times, admission prices and other details.

Melford Hall

Long Melford, Sudbury CO10 9AH
Tel. Sudbury (0787) 880286
In Long Melford on E side of A134, 14m S of Bury St Edmunds, 3m
of Sudbury

Melford was built by the shrewd Tudor lawyer, Sir Willia
Cordell, in the middle of the sixteenth century and the outsi
of the house looks much the same as it did four hundred yea
ago. The inside of the house has not fared so well. It w
ransacked during the Civil War and there was a disastrous fire
1942. Despite this you can still find many associations with tl
Cordell family and with the seafaring Parker family who boug
the hall in 1786.

Don't Miss...

● The Tudor Great Hall which
rises through two storeys
of the house.

● The 5th Baronet ran away from
school to join the merchant navy and
worked his way up through the ranks to
become a highly skilled admiral. In
1762 he captured a Spanish galleon
loaded with presents from the Emperor
of Peking to the King of Spain – the
Chinese porcelain around the house are
the spoils from this raid.

The 5th baronet ran
away from school t
join the merchant n

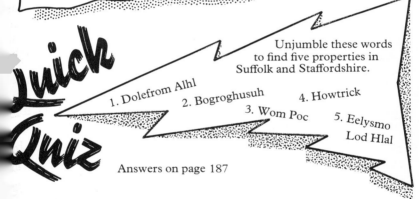

- Three members of the Parker family were admirals and the pictures in the library show some of the experiences they had at sea.

- Beatrix Potter's cousin married the 10th Baronet and Beatrix often used to visit Melford. There is an exhibition about this famous children's author in the room where she used to stay, with many of her pictures. Melford Hall featured in one of her books, **The Fox and the Stork**.

Quick Quiz

Unjumble these words to find five properties in Suffolk and Staffordshire.

1. Dolefrom Alhl   2. Bogroghusuh   4. Howtrick

3. Wom Poc   5. Eelysmo Lod Hlal

Answers on page 187

Surrey

Countryside

The Trust owns or protects about 13,500 acres in Surrey, so there's plenty to explore.

The 1,000 acres of heath and woodland at Frensham Common near Farnham is part of a country park with a special conservation walk to try out.

● Witley Common near Milford is rich in wildlife and birds. A[x] information centre supplies leaflets telling you what to look ou[x] for when walking on the common. There are also several natur[x] trails.

● At Hindhead there are more than 1,400 acres of heathland an[x] woodland with nature walks to help you discover more about th[x] countryside. The area has fascinating place names such as th[x] Devil's Punchbowl and Gibbet Hill where criminals wer[x] hanged. You can see right across the Weald to the South Downs[x]

● Most of the 360 acres of open down, copse and beechwoo[x] above Reigate was bought with money raised by local people[x] There are walks through Reigate Beeches, the wood at Gatto[x] Park and marvellous views from Colley and Juniper hills.

● The Trust owns a 20-mile stretch of the River Wey betwee[x] Godalming and Weybridge. It used to be busy with barge[x] carrying grain and timber to London but once the railways cam[x] the river lost its importance as a means of transport. You can ge[x] down to the towpath at lots of different points along its route[x] watch the locks working, fish, go canoeing, birdwatch, or jus[x] enjoy following the river along the towpath.

Remember to consult **The National Trust Handbook** for opening times, admission prices and other details.

BOX TREE

Box Hill

Tel. Dorking (0306) 885502 for general enquiries
1m N of Dorking, 2½m S of Leatherhead on A24

This 800-acre area of woodland and downland has lots of different species of wild flowering plants and butterflies to look out for.

Don't Miss...

● Follow some of the nature trails and visit the exhibition room for more information on this lovely area.

● Have a look at the nineteenth-century fort at the top of the hill.

● Look for a stone on the north-west brow of the hill. This is said to mark the grave of Major Peter Labellière who asked to be buried standing on his head, so that when the world turned upside down at the resurrection he'd end up standing on his feet!

The 4th Earl finds he is heir to no more than a shell.

Clandon Park

West Clandon, Guildford GU4 7RQ
Tel. Guildford (0483) 222482
At West Clandon on A247, 3m E of Guildford on A424

Clandon House was built *c*.1731 for the 2nd Baron Onslow by the Italian architect Giacomo Leoni. When the 4th Earl of Onslow inherited the house in 1870 it was in a bad way and suffering from almost fifty years of neglect: the chimneys were full of bird's nests, the pipes had all burst and no repairs or painting had been done for years. He managed to rescue the house from any further decay, restored it and made it the Onslow family home again.

Don't Miss...

● The Maori meeting house in the garden brought back from New Zealand by the 4th Earl who was Governor of New Zealand from 1888 to 1892. There is a room in the house with lots of other objects from New Zealand, including a Maori chief's feather cloak.

● If you want to see a ceiling with legs look up in Clandon's marble hall! It's the most incredible 3D plaster ceiling with larger than life human figures.

● There are birds all over the house – in paintings, carved in wood on the staircase, sticking out of the wall as light brackets and stuffed in cases. Look out for the rare collection of porcelain birds from China – some of the pieces are over three hundred years old. They were collected by Mrs David Gubbay who spent her childhood in India surrounded by exotic birds – including a mynah bird trained to sing the national anthem.

Claremont Landscape Garden

Portsmouth Road, Esher
On S edge of Esher, on E side of A307

Claremont Landscape Garden was worked on by some of the greatest landscape gardeners of the eighteenth century – Bridgeman, Kent, Vanbrugh and Capability Brown – and was famous throughout Europe.

Don't Miss...

● The grotto at the end of the lake and the amphitheatre made out of grass, with its five rows of seating forming a semi-circle around the stage.

● Claremont House (not open) was built by Vanbrugh, and was lived in by Clive of India, so the garden restaurant serves dishes with Indian themes. The house was also home to Princess Charlotte: the only daughter of George IV, she died tragically in childbirth. The railings outside the camellia house are decorated with crowns and L's, the initial of her husband, Leopold of Saxe-Coburg.

● There are lots of different paths through the garden to explore to find the different views created in the landscape.

Hatchlands

East Clandon, Guildford GU4 7RT
Tel. Guildford (0483) 222787
E of East Clandon, N of A246 Guildford–Leatherhead road

Admiral Edward Boscawen built Hatchlands in the 1750s with money he won for beating the French in several naval battles.

Don't Miss...

● The famous eighteenth-century architect, Robert Adam, was asked to decorate some of the rooms. You can see the nautical theme running through his work: mermaids, sea-horses, dolphins and anchors all appear.

● There are extensive grounds with an ice house and a temple to explore.

● The Cobbe collection of keyboard instruments in the house is on loan to the Trust. There is even a harpsichord made for Marie Antoinette which escaped damage in the French Revolution. Concerts are often held at the house so that the instruments can be heard as well as seen.

A FRENCH HARPSICHORD ESCAPING FROM THE REVOLUTION

Leith Hill Tower

Tel. Dorking (0306) 712434
On summit of Leith Hill, 1m SW of Coldharbour on A29/B2126

Leith Hill Tower stands on top of the highest point of south-east England. This Gothic folly was built in 1766 by Richard Hull who is buried on the spot.

Don't Miss...

● The amazing views from the tower. When you stand at the top you are 1,029 feet above sea level and on a clear day you can see the Channel through the Shoreham Gap of the South Downs.

● Explore the heath and woodland around the Tower. It is an Area of Outstanding Natural Beauty and maps of the property and nature walks are on sale at the Tower Tea Kiosk.

Polesden Lacey

Near Dorking RH5 6BD
Tel. Bookham (0372) 58203
3m W of Dorking, 1½m S of Great Bookham off
A246 Leatherhead–Guildford road.

Some of the most famous people of the early twentieth century
were invited to stay at Polesden Lacey – the Queen Mother even
spent part of her honeymoon here! It was the home of Mrs
Ronald Greville, a society hostess who loved entertaining the
rich and famous and who bought the house for this purpose in
1906.

MENU

Don't Miss...

- The mementoes kept by Mrs Greville as a record of her guests. You can even find out what they ate when they stayed there from the menu book.

- The house is filled with valuable paintings and objects, most of which Mrs Greville had inherited from her father who founded McEwan's brewery.

- There are lots of different parts of the garden and grounds to explore including an enormous rose garden crammed with different varieties. Mrs Greville was so fond of the house and garden that she asked to be buried just outside the rose garden. She was also devoted to her pet dogs and they are buried in the grounds as well.

- Find the stone griffins keeping guard in front of the house.

- There is a Youth Hostel on the estate.

East Sussex

Bateman's

Burwash, Etchingham TN19 7DS
Tel. Burwash (0435) 882302
S of Burwash off A265

Bateman's was probably built for a local ironmaster in the late
seventeenth century but most people visit the house because it
was the home of the great writer Rudyard Kipling from 1902 to
1936. Try to read some of his books like **The Jungle Book** or
Just So Stories before you visit.

Don't Miss...

● Kipling's study is exactly as he left it. His pipe lies in the ashtray and his pen sits waiting for him to pick it up and start writing again. Kipling was a perfectionist, the huge wastepaper bin was where he would throw away any of his writing which did not meet his high standards. From the study window you can see a hill, the setting for Kipling's book, **Puck of Pook's Hill**.

● Kipling spent his childhood in India and the Oriental rugs, objects and paintings around the house are all reminders of the happy years he spent there.

● The mill in the grounds is now restored to working order and you can see flour being ground here.

● Kipling loved driving – his vintage 1928 Rolls Royce still stands in the garage.

Bodiam Castle

Bodiam, near Robertsbridge TN32 5UA
Tel. Staplecross (058 083) 436
3m S of Hawkhurst, 1m E of A229

Bodiam must be one of the few castles which was never attacke
It was begun in 1385 to defend the area from the possibility
invading French forces. By the time the building was finish
the French had been defeated at sea at the Battle of Margate a
were no longer a threat.

Don't Miss...

● Explore the castle and imagine what it was like when it was fully furnished.

● The owner, Sir Edward Dalyngrigge, made sure that Bodiam was comfortable to live in as well as properly defended. There are remains of fireplaces and carved windows, and each of the main bedrooms had a garderobe (lavatory).

● There are audio-visual presentations in the castle describing what life was like in medieval times and how a suit of armour was worn; there is also a museum.

West Sussex

The Trust owns and protects about 13,000 acres of coas and countryside in West Sussex. Here are just a few places you could visit.

Black Down, 1 mile south east of Haslemere, is the highes point in Sussex with fine views to the South Downs and th English Channel. There is also interesting birdlife to look for linnets, yellowhammers, woodpeckers, warblers and tree pipits

Highdown Hill, 3 miles north west of Worthing, is a important archaeological site, and finds from the site are now i the Worthing Museum.

Slindon Park Estate, 6 miles north of Bognor Regis. Thi 3,520-acre estate consists of farm, woodland, park and part the village of Slindon. There are plenty of walks in the park an footpaths on the estate to explore, including $3\frac{1}{2}$ miles of Stan Street, the Roman road from London to Chichester which now a bridleway.

Petworth Park is a beautiful 700-acre deer park landscaped b Capability Brown. It is the setting for the seventeenth-centu Petworth House which is also owned by the Trust.

Standden

East Grinstead RH19 4NE
Tel. East Grinstead (0342) 323029
2m S of East Grinstead

Standen was built for James Beale, a wealthy London solicitor, who wanted a country retreat. Designed by the architect Philip Webb the house shows the value he placed on good quality materials and craftsmanship. The result is a comfortable and friendly house decorated by the top designers of the day.

Don't Miss...

● William Morris, the artist craftsman, designed the wallpaper and furnishing fabrics – you may recognise some of them as his designs are still very popular today.

● Although the house has twelve bedrooms there is only one bathroom!

● The Billiard Room with its racks for cues and balls.

● There are acres of gardens to explore on the steep south-facing slope. You can see the quarry where the stone to build the house came from.

Quick Quiz

1. Where will you find Mowgli and friends in the Sussex countryside?
2. Where did the Queen Mother spend part of her honeymoon?
3. Who stands on his head under a box in Surrey?

Answers on page 187

Tyne and Wear

The Leas and Marsden Rock

South Shields
South Shields–Sunderland road E of A183

There are three miles of spectacular coastline owned by the Trust between Trow Rocks and Lizard Point. The limestone cliffs have been worn away by the weather and sea to produce varied coastline with caves and coves and the enormous arch through Marden Rock. There are also sandy beaches.

INFORMATION

Don't Miss...

● The area is famous for its birds and if you're there at the right time of year you might see cormorants, fulmars and kittiwakes.

● There is an information cabin at Marsden Grotto car park where you can find out more about the geology and birdlife of the area.

● There are guided walks with the warden from May to August.

Warwickshire

Baddesley Clinton

nowle, Solihull B93 0DQ
l. Lapworth (056 43) 3294
W of A41 Warwick–Birmingham road at Chadwick End

he Ferrers family lived at this medieval moated manor house
om the early sixteenth century until the beginning of the
cond World War in 1939. They were devout Catholics and
e house became a sanctuary for many Catholics on the run
om religious persecution in the sixteenth century. The family
is fined heavily for its religious beliefs, leaving little money to
end on the house; consequently it has changed little in its four
undred years.

Don't Miss...

The stained glass, commissioned in the
xteenth century by Henry Ferrers, which
aces the different coats of arms of his
ncestors.

The house has several secret hiding places
here fleeing Catholics could shelter. One is
ade out of an old drain in the kitchen. In
)ctober 1591 nine men escaped capture by
iding here, with their feet in water for
our hours!

The moat dates back to the thirteenth
entury and the only way into the house is
ver its single bridge.

Family ticket available.

Charlecote Park

Wellesbourne, Warwick CV35 9ER
Tel. Stratford-upon-Avon (0789) 470277
1m W of Wellesbourne, 5m E of Stratford-upon-Avon,
6m S of Warwick on N side of B4086

Charlecote has been the home of the Lucy family since 1247 although the present house was built in the 1550s. Queen Elizabeth I visited Charlecote and Shakespeare is said to have poached deer from the park!

Don't Miss...

● Go into the kitchens and imagine what it would have been like to work there. There was no running water, no food storage cupboards, no chairs, no tins, packets or frozen food – but there was a cook who ruled a staff of fifteen with a rod of iron. Look for the handpump in the scullery, the dry store for grain, the still room for bottled pickles and fruit, the fish store, and the dairy where milk was churned into butter and cheese. Although a coal-fired range was put into the kitchen in 1880, the open hearth was kept in use so that a whole sheep or deer could be roasted.

● You can see a video of life in Victorian times at Charlecote.

● The summerhouse in the park, known as Granny's Summerhouse, was built for the children by the butler in 1860, and is furnished with beautiful miniature antiques.

● The park was landscaped by the famous gardener, Capability Brown. There are herds of red and fallow deer, and Jacob sheep have been kept in the park since 1756.

44

● Try to read **The Children of Charlecote** by Philippa Pearce and Brian Fairfax-Lucy. This is set in the years leading up to the First World War and tells the true story of the life of the Lucy children at Charlecote.

● Family ticket available.

Coughton Court

Near Alcester B49 5JA
Tel. Alcester (0789) 762435
2m N of Alcester on E side of A435

Coughton Court has been owned by a family of staunch Catholics, the Throckmortons, since 1409. Like many Catholics, the family suffered for its faith. Sir Nicholas Throckmorton was imprisoned by Elizabeth I for his friendship with Mary Queen of Scots, and his nephew was executed for plotting against the queen. Coughton was also where the men behind the Gunpowder Plot planned their scheme to blow up James I and the Houses of Parliament.

Don't Miss...

● During times of religious persecution the Throckmortons made sure that the Catholic mass was still celebrated. There were several hiding places for priests in the house. When the north-east turret was opened in 1870 a rope ladder, a bed and folding leather altar were found there.

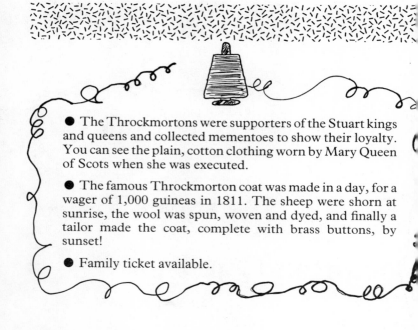

- The Throckmortons were supporters of the Stuart kings and queens and collected mementoes to show their loyalty. You can see the plain, cotton clothing worn by Mary Queen of Scots when she was executed.

- The famous Throckmorton coat was made in a day, for a wager of 1,000 guineas in 1811. The sheep were shorn at sunrise, the wool was spun, woven and dyed, and finally a tailor made the coat, complete with brass buttons, by sunset!

- Family ticket available.

Packwood House

Lapworth, Solihull B94 6AT
Tel. Lapworth (056 43) 2024
On A34 2m W of Hockley Heath

Packwood House was built for the Fetherston family at the end of the sixteenth century. Although most families were supporters of either the Royalists or the Parliamentarians during the Civil War, some families would appear neutral and support whichever side suited the occasion. There are tales of households having huge oak chests with 'God save the King' carved on one side and 'God save the Commonwealth' on the other. This might have been the case with the Fetherston family who, it is said, gave shelter to one of Cromwell's generals on the night before the Battle of Edgehill and provided the same hospitality for Charles II after his defeat at the Battle of Worcester!

Don't Miss...

● Many of the pieces of furniture in the house were sold to the Fetherstons by their neighbours, the Ferrers family of Baddesley Clinton (see p.143). The Ferrers were staunch Catholics and were fined heavily for their faith. They had to resort to selling some of their possessions as a result of crippling fines.

● The wonderful yew garden. These yew trees are said to have been planted to represent the Sermon on the Mount. Can you find the twelve Apostles, the four Evangelists and the single yew on the hummock which represents Christ?

● Family ticket available.

Upton House

anbury, Oxfordshire OX15 6HT
el. Edge Hill (029 587) 266
n A422, 7m NW of Banbury, 12m SE of Stratford-upon-Avon

pton House is famous for its collection of paintings, tapestries, ghteenth-century furniture, china and porcelain. This valu-le collection was acquired over the years by Walter Samuel, nd Lord Bearsted, who was not only a passionate art collector ut was also a generous benefactor and gave much of his money way to hospitals, schools and charities. He bought Upton in 927 and remodelled and extended the building in order to ouse his works of art.

Don't Miss...

● Even if you don't think you're interested in art, it's definitely worth taking time to wander round the house and look at Lord Bearsted's wonderful collections – you might have changed your mind by the time you've finished! Nearly everything you see in the house was personally chosen by him and shows what a wide taste in all types of art he had.

● The garden is very varied and worth exploring. It is thought that the neatly laid out kitchen garden has been a source of fruit and vegetables to Upton House for over three hundred years.

● The largest of the original four stew ponds which would have once supplied the household with fish lies at the foot of the kitchen garden. It is now stocked with golden orfe.

● If you visit in the spring make sure you walk through Blackwell's Wood and see the mass of bluebells.

Wiltshire

Avebury

Near Marlborough SN8 1RF
6m W of Marlborough, 1m N of the A4 at junction of A361 and B400.

Avebury stone circle was built in about BC 2500, although, lik many prehistoric remains, no one can be sure what it was buil for.

Don't Miss...

● There are at least 180 stones weighing between 15 and 45 tons each and some stand over 20 feet high. These stones would have been brought from 25 miles away.

● The 30-acre area enclosed by the stones is surrounded by an enormous circular ditch which would have been dug by hand using antler picks and shovels made out of ox shoulder blades. The people working on this ditch dug out 200,000 tons of chalk!

● There is a museum by the church where you can find out more about this 4,500-year-old mystery.

● The circle has suffered over the years. Medieval villagers were suspicious of its pagan connections and tried to bury and burn many of the stones. Later on, in the nineteenth century, more of the boulders were broken up for building materials.

● There is a museum run by English Heritage explaining the excavation of the area.

● The Great Barn in the village has an exhibition of Wiltshire rural life and is run by the Wiltshire Folk Life Society.

Fox Talbot Museum and Lacock Village

Lacock, near Chippenham SN15 2LG
Tel. Lacock (0249) 73459
Lacock, 3m S of Chippenham, just E of A350

*in village

Henry Fox Talbot was one of the leading pioneers in the invention of photography and at the Fox Talbot Museum you can find out all about this man and his part in the history of photography.

Don't Miss...

● You can see some of the very first attempts at photography in the museum. There is a tiny print of an oriel window at Lacock Abbey which Fox Talbot made from the world's first negative.

● You can also see the camera he used to take this photo: he called it a 'mousetrap' camera and it was made by the village carpenter.

● Take time to walk around the pretty village of Lacock and Lacock Abbey, Fox Talbot's home which was built around the remains of a Cistercian convent.

Stourhead Garden

Stourton, Warminster BA12 6QH
Tel. Bourton (0747) 840348
At Stourton off B3092, 3m NW of Mere

*in Spread Eagle Inn
†only Nov to end Feb

Henry Hoare, a wealthy banker, was responsible for commissioning one of Britain's most famous landscape gardens. Stourhead Garden was laid out between 1741 and 1780 and is full of surprises.

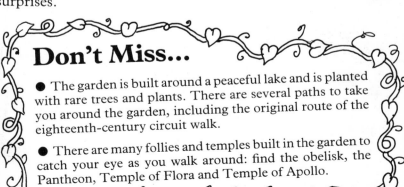

Don't Miss...

● The garden is built around a peaceful lake and is planted with rare trees and plants. There are several paths to take you around the garden, including the original route of the eighteenth-century circuit walk.

● There are many follies and temples built in the garden to catch your eye as you walk around: find the obelisk, the Pantheon, Temple of Flora and Temple of Apollo.

The grotto with the statue of a water god.

North Yorkshire

Countryside

ver 17,000 acres of countryside and coastline are owned and protected by the Trust in North Yorkshire.

● At Ravenscar you can follow a geological trail to find out more about how the area was formed. There are also guided walks, so find out from the Ravenscar National Trust Coastal Centre when they take place.

● Clayton Bay has a very popular broad stretch of beach. The area is a mass of different habitats so you can explore the sandy and rocky shoreline or go further inland to find the area's woods and ponds.

Upper Wharfedale, 8 miles north of Grassington, consists of
_00 acres of magnificent Dales landscape with lots of foot-
ths to help you explore this beautiful area.

The Malham Tarn Estate, 6 miles north east of Settle, covers
_00 acres and includes Ewe Moor, a dry limestone valley
_ve Malham Cove. The tarn and its wetlands are an important
ture reserve where you can see wheatears, curlews, lapwings
d redshanks. On the tarn itself there are coots, tufted ducks
d great crested grebes. Malham Tarn was the inspiration for
_arles Kingsley's book, **The Water Babies**. You can only
_ch the tarn by foot and the walk up from Malham village is
_ough some eerie limestone landscape.

This part of Yorkshire is rich in weird geological formations:
_imham Rocks and Moor, 8 miles south west of Ripon, is
_vered with millstone grit stacks eroded into fantastic shapes
_ thousands of years of weathering. Many of the stacks have
_mes: Dancing Bear, the Idol, Druid's Writing Desk and the
_boon's Head. There is a leaflet available with a plan giving
_mes of the rocks.

DRUID'S
WRITING
DESK

● You can also see the Bridestones on the moor 12 miles south
Whitby. These are huge Jurassic sandstone slabs which a
wider at the top than the bottom. Through thousands of years
overweathering, lower layers of softer rock have worn away at
faster rate than the harder upper layers. The two largest stac
are called the Pepper Pot and Salt Cellar. There is a leafl
available showing you how to get to these formations and telli
you what plants, trees and wildlife to look out for on the way

Beningbrough Hall

Shipton-by-Beningbrough, York YO6 1DD
Tel. York (0904) 470666
8m NW of York, 2m W of Shipton

Massive restoration work was needed when the National Tru
took over this imposing Georgian house. It took nearly thr
years and an enormous amount of hard work to make the hou
and stables what they are today. Henry VIII granted t
Beningbrough estate to John Banister in 1544. The estate the
passed to his daughter's and son-in-law's family, the Bou
chiers. The original Elizabethan house was pulled down and t
house you see now was built for John Bourchier and finished
1716.

Don't Miss...

● The display of eighteenth-century portraits lent by the
National Portrait Gallery.

● The fully equipped Victorian laundry where you can see
how people coped before the days of washing machines and
tumble driers.

154

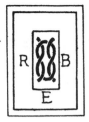

● The decorative woodcarvings by William Thornton. You should be able to see John Bourchier's initials carved in various places around the house.

● The corner chimneypieces built with stepped shelving to display oriental porcelain. This was a Dutch fashion and became popular in England when William and Mary were on the throne.

● Beningbrough would have had a large staff of gardeners to look after the grounds and the kitchen garden, providing the house with vegetables and flowers throughout the year. Don't miss the Victorian potting shed.

● As well as having a wilderness play area and a walled garden suitable for outdoor games, Beningbrough holds many family events in the school holidays. There are also Christmas carol concerts.

● Try the Larch Walk and visit the pike ponds.

● Family ticket available.

Remember to consult **The National Trust Handbook** for opening times, admission prices and other details.

Fountains Abbey and Studley Royal

Fountains, Ripon HG4 3DZ
Tel. Sawley (076 586) 333
4m W of Ripon off B626

Fountains Abbey, on the banks of the River Skell, was found
by Cistercian monks in 1132 and is the largest monastic ruin
Britain. The abbey was abandoned at the Dissolution of t
Monasteries, but in the eighteenth century it took on a differe
role as a romantic and ruined focus point in a grand landscap
water garden, the creation of John and William Aislabie. T
gardens and the abbey have survived.

Don't Miss...

● There are many surviving remains from the abbey to
give clues about the monks' way of life. The stone pedestals
which used to support the monks' tables still stand on the
floor, now grassy, of the refectory. You can also see the
cunningly constructed serving hatches for getting the food.

● The abbey would have been very cold. There was one
heated room in the whole place where the monks could
toast their feet for a brief hour each day!

● The monks led a strict life. Find the remains of the
parlour where talking was allowed for a brief spell.

● Some say the abbey is haunted and that occasionally a
ghostly choir of monks can be heard chanting in the Chapel
of the Nine Altars.

If you sit in Anne Boleyn's seat you will get a surprise!

● The gardens of Studley Royal were built in two parts: first as a formal water garden, and then developed to take in the surrounding areas. There are walks around the park so you can see some of the follies and appreciate the views. If you sit in Anne Boleyn's seat you'll get an unexpected view of the abbey.

● Family ticket available.

Mount Grace Priory

Osmotherley, Northallerton DL6 3JG
Tel. Osmotherley (060 983) 494
m NE of Northallerton, ½m E off A19

🚽 ♿ ★ 🏕 🐕 wc

The ruins of the fourteenth-century priory of Mount Grace will
give you an insight into the lives of the members of one of the
strictest religious orders, the Carthusians. These monks not

only lived a life of isolation from the outside world but also ha
little contact with each other. The Priory is managed by Englis
Heritage.

Don't Miss...

● Stone walls outline the remains of 24 of the monks' cells. Each cell was self-contained, with a private study, bedroom, workroom, garderobe (lavatory) and garden. One cell has been reconstructed to show the conditions in which the monks lived.

● The monks would spend most of their time praying, copying out religious works and living lives of contemplation. They would only see each other on Sundays and feastdays when the tiny church would be used.

● On some of the cells the hatch through which food was served still exists. A right-angled bend was built into the cell so that the monk and server would not see each other.

Nunnington Hall

Nunnington, York YO6 5UY
Tel. Nunnington (043 95) 283
In Ryedale, 4½m SE of Helmsley off A170

Nunnington was the home of Richard Graham, 1st Viscou
Preston, who inherited the estate in 1685. Preston was a
important member of James II's government and was one of fiv
men to whom James handed over the ruling of the country whe
he fled to France in 1688. Preston had a plan to sail to Franc

d bring James back in triumph – unfortunately he was caught
rrying incriminating papers and although his valet helped him
y swallowing some of these, Preston was sent to the Tower of
ondon. He was saved from execution by the pleadings of his
aughter, Susannah, and returned to Nunnington.

MINIATURE ANTIQUE SHOP

Don't Miss...

● The unique Carlisle Collection of Miniature Rooms set
out in the attic. These intricate rooms, an eighth of actual
size, are decorated in styles of different ages and crammed
with detail.

● The family bedrooms, the nursery and the maids'
rooms.

● The gardens have been restored to reflect the different
periods of gardening styles from the sixteenth and seventeenth centuries.

West Yorkshire

East Riddlesden Hall

Bradford Road, Keighley BD20 5EL
Tel. Keighley (0535) 607075
1m NE of Keighley on S side of A650

This seventeenth-century manor house was saved from derelic-
tion in the 1930s. The Trust has refurnished the house and it
now gives a good idea of what everyday life would have been like
in the seventeenth century.

Don't Miss...

● The furniture is mostly locally made, some of it is very
unusual. Look out for the shepherd's chair, built with a
hutch underneath it to hold a dog or a lamb.

● The Hall is said to have many ghosts. One of them is the
Lady in White who was thrown from her horse and
drowned in the ancient fish pond. Another is the Grey
Lady, who is said to have been locked up in her room to
starve to death by her husband after he found her with
another man.

● There is a 120-foot long medieval barn with a fascinating collection of old farm machinery.

● There are regular special events for children at the Hall,
including the Riddlesden Revels on the first Sunday of
each month and Christmas carol concerts. Telephone for
more details.

Wales: Clwyd

Chirk Castle

Chirk LL14 5AF
Tel. Chirk (0691) 777701
½ W of Chirk village off A5

In the Middle Ages, King Edward I started a massive programme of castle building in an attempt to subdue the Welsh. In 1295 Roger Mortimer began to construct Castell-y-Waun, which means 'Meadow Castle' in Welsh. The castle is now called Chirk, and although from the outside it still looks like a medieval fortress, inside it has been transformed into an elegant country home by the Myddelton family who have lived there for almost 400 years.

Don't Miss...

● The gloomy castle dungeon hollowed out of the rock. The only way to reach it is by a spiral staircase set into the 15-foot thick walls. Only two narrow beams of light would have reached anyone imprisoned here.

● The 93-foot deep well in the castle courtyard.

● The castle is set in a large park. Some of the trees here were planted during Charles II's reign, more than three hundred years ago.

● The unusual thatched hawk house in the garden and the hue topiary yew hedge, cut to make it look like a castle wall with the battlements.

● There is a family ticket available.

Erddig

Near Wrexham, Clwyd LL13 0YT
Tel. Wrexham (0978) 355314
2m S of Wrexham

When Erddig was given to the National Trust in 1973 it wa
literally falling apart. However, this fine seventeenth-centur
house, the home of the Yorke family, was a special place. It no
only had a wonderful collection of eighteenth-century fur
niture, but it also contained a vast amount of information abou
what life was like for servants at the house and workers on th
estate. This window into life 'below stairs' was worth preservin
at all costs.

Don't Miss...

● Visit the kitchens, blacksmith's forge, sawmill, laundry, bakehouse and joinery.

● The Yorke family had paintings and photographs made of their servants and wrote poems about them. In the Servants' Hall see if you can find Sarah Davies, a dairy maid who worked at the house in the middle of the nineteenth-century – 'in everything she well did please, save in the art of making cheese'.

● A 10-minute video shows the restoration of Erddig. It is hard to believe now that water poured in, ceilings bulged, wallpaper hung in tatters and the garden was a jungle.

Dyfed

Countryside

The Pembrokeshire Coastal footpath is 168 miles long. It starts at Amroth on Carmarthen Bay and ends at St Dogmaels, just outside Cardigan. Most of this path travels through National Trust property. Here are a few places to visit along this wild and beautiful stretch of coastline.

From Kete, west of Dale, there is a good walk to the cliffs of St Anne's Head where you can see the bird sanctuary islands of Skomer and Skokholm. The islands (not NT) can be reached by boat from St David's.

RAZORBILL

● The Trust owns about 15½ miles of coastline at St Bride's Ba
Try the 2½-mile walk from Marloes Sands which will take yo
past the sandstone cliffs, an Iron Age fort and Marloes Mer
You may also be able to see seals basking along the coast.

● There are good bathing beaches at Mwnt between Cardiga
and Newquay, and at Penbryn, north-east of Tresaith.

Dolaucothi Gold Mines

Pumsaint, Llanwrda SA19 8RR
Tel. Pumsaint (055 85) 359
Between Lampeter and Llanwrda on A482

Gold mining began at Dolaucothi nearly 2,000 years ago whe
the Romans started mining the area. The mines were la
worked in 1938.

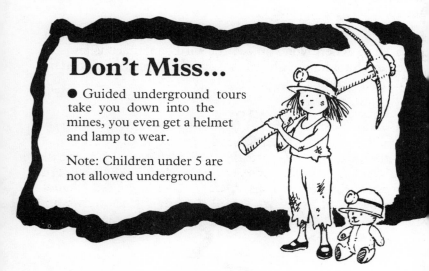

Don't Miss...

● Guided underground tours take you down into the mines, you even get a helmet and lamp to wear.

Note: Children under 5 are not allowed underground.

- Follow the Miners' Way Trail and find out more about the history of the mines. There are tunnels as well as open-cast sites. You can still see the pick marks in the rocks left by slaves working for their Roman masters.

- A collection of 1930s mining equipment gives an idea of how the mines were worked earlier this century.

- An audio-visual show tells you about the history of gold mining at Dolaucothi.

Stackpole Estate

Near Pembroke
m S of Pembroke on B4319

Take a 2,000-acre mix of cliffs, woodlands, seashore and lakes; add an abundance of wildlife including herons, seals and puffins; stir in fascinating rock formations such as blow holes and stacks and you have Stackpole, one of the most beautiful and varied estates in Wales.

Stackpole was once owned by the Campbells, the Earls of Cawdor in Scotland. Two hundred years ago they transformed the landscape by planting great numbers of trees, damming the valleys to make lakes, and moved Stackpole village out of sight of Stackpole Court, the family house. The house was demolished in 1962 but the estate is still there for you to enjoy and explore.

Don't Miss...

● There are plenty of waymarked trails to help you find your way around the estate.

● The freshwater lakes at Bosherton. These were created by the Cawdors for boating and fishing and were stocked with roach, perch, pike and tench. In summer they are covered with waterlilies.

● Walk over the headland from Stackpole Quay to Barafundle Bay with its golden sand and good swimming conditions. There is also a good beach at Broad Haven, sheltered by low cliffs and backed by sand dunes.

● The Old Quarry at Stackpole has been turned into an adventure area. There is an archery bay and the rocks have been cleared for climbing and abseiling. Telephone Castlemartin (064681) 359 to find out how you can join in these activities.

Gwynedd

The Lleyn Peninsula

The Lleyn Peninsula divides Caernarfon Bay from Cardigan Bay and is a wild and beautiful area to explore.

Don't Miss...

● At Mynydd-y-Graig is an ancient hill fort standing 800 feet above the sea with uninterrupted views south across Cardigan Bay and the Irish Sea.

● From the headland of Mynydd Penarfynydd you can see the Gwylan Islands which are home to a large number of puffins.

● The cove at Porth Llanllawen below Mynydd Analog where grey seals breed.

● The cliffs on this peninsula are home to many birds and you should easily see gulls, fulmars and ravens. The chough, a bird which has become extinct in Cornwall, has survived in this area.

Penrhyn Castle

Near Bangor LL57 4HN
Tel. Bangor (0248) 353084
1m E of Bangor at Llandegai on A5122

Penrhyn Castle looks just like an eleventh-century Norman castle but is in fact a house, built between 1820 and 1845 at a time when it was fashionable to build in the 'Norman' style. It was commissioned by G.H. Dawkins Pennant who spent the profits from the Penrhyn slate quarries on his grand new home.

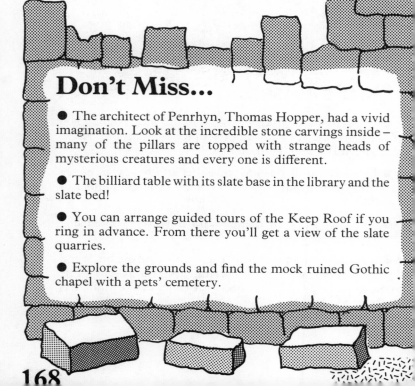

Don't Miss...

● The architect of Penrhyn, Thomas Hopper, had a vivid imagination. Look at the incredible stone carvings inside – many of the pillars are topped with strange heads of mysterious creatures and every one is different.

● The billiard table with its slate base in the library and the slate bed!

● You can arrange guided tours of the Keep Roof if you ring in advance. From there you'll get a view of the slate quarries.

● Explore the grounds and find the mock ruined Gothic chapel with a pets' cemetery.

- In the stables is a museum displaying locomotives and trucks once used in the slate quarries, a model railway, and a large collection of dolls from all over the world.

- There is an Adventurers' Audio Tour (in Welsh and English) available to enliven your trip around the house.

- Explore the servants' quarters and find the soup tower where the estate workers were fed.

- Family ticket available.

Plas Newydd

Llanfairpwll, Anglesey LL61 6EQ
Tel. Llanfairpwll (0248) 714795
In SW of Llanfairpwll and A5 on A4080

Plas Newydd is a fascinating house dominated by the work of the artist, Rex Whistler, who was killed in the Second World War. The 6th Marquess of Anglesey, who owned Plas Newydd, was Whistler's patron and commissioned him to paint a huge seascape mural in the Dining Room.

Don't Miss...

- You could spend hours looking at the mural in the Dining Room as it is full of detail. The man sweeping up leaves is a self-portrait of Whistler. Find the footsteps of Neptune in the painting.

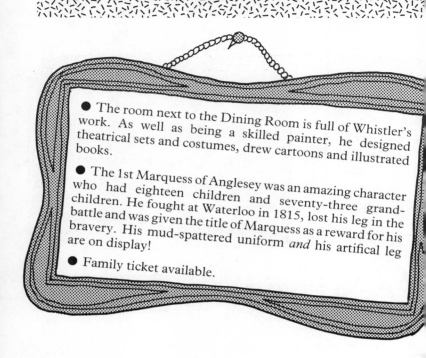

● The room next to the Dining Room is full of Whistler's work. As well as being a skilled painter, he designed theatrical sets and costumes, drew cartoons and illustrated books.

● The 1st Marquess of Anglesey was an amazing character who had eighteen children and seventy-three grand-children. He fought at Waterloo in 1815, lost his leg in the battle and was given the title of Marquess as a reward for his bravery. His mud-spattered uniform *and* his artifical leg are on display!

● Family ticket available.

Segontium

Caernarfon
Tel. Caernarfon (0286) 5625
On A4085 on SE outskirts of Caernarfon

Built about 78 AD, the fort of Segontium was one of over 30 tha the Romans built to control the rebellious tribes in the valley west of the rivers Severn and Dee. The Romans held this fo until 390, longer than any other fort in Wales. Some of the stor used for building Edward I's castle at Caernarfon was take from here.

Don't Miss...

● The remains of the underfloor heating system for the main headquarters in the centre of the site.

● The basic bath suite which would have had to cater for up to 1,000 soldiers!

● The museum describing Segontium and what life would have been like in the Roman army.

● Segontium is in the care of Cadw: Welsh Historic Monuments and is managed by the National Museum of Wales.

Powys

Powis Castle

Welshpool SY21 8RF
Tel. Welshpool (0938) 4336
1 S of Welshpool on A483

Built around 1200 by the Welsh princes, this romantic castle is perched high on a rock on a marvellous defensive site. The Herbert family have lived in the castle since 1587 with one break in 1688 during the Glorious Revolution, when William Herbert fled with James II to France.

Don't Miss...

● The original castle has been extended over the years. Try to find out when the additions were made.

● The Clive Museum. One of the Herbert daughters married the eldest son of Clive of India in 1784 and many of the family's Indian treasures, such as a solid gold tiger's head, are on display next to the Ballroom.

● Powis is famous for its terraced gardens packed with flowers and shrubs and shaped yew trees. Take time to explore the grounds.

● A medieval wooded deer park surrounds the castle and has ancient oaks which may be over 800 years old. There have been black cattle in the park since the Middle Ages.

● Family ticket available.

West Glamorgan

Countryside

The Trust owns 5,000 acres of the beautiful Gower Peninsula with its sandy beaches, cliffs, caves and birdlife. Try to visit some of the Trust's land in this area.

Rhossili Down – the highest hill on the Gower. On a clear day you can see as far as Devon. There are two megalithic tombs thought to be associated with the Viking sealord, Sweyn, who probably gave his name to Swansea.

Rhossili Bay – this 5-mile-long beach is worth visiting, especially if you like fishing or surfing. Look out for: the Iron Age earthworks and the ruins of a medieval church at the Burry Holn end of the bay; the wild flowers on the cliffs; and the timber ribs of the **Helvetia** poking out of the sand, a reminder of the boat wrecked in 1887.

Worms Head – this thin promontory gets its name from the old English word for Dragon, 'wurm'. It's an area where many important archaeological finds have been made: bones of mammoths, woolly rhinoceroses and reindeer have been found in one cave and at Paviland Cave the 'Red Lady' skeleton was found (it was later discovered that the skeleton was a man!). Find the Devil's Bridge, an archway of rocks formed by sea and wind erosion.

WORMS HEAD

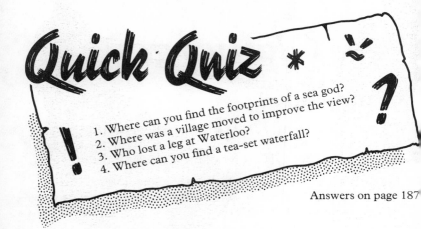

Quick Quiz *

1. Where can you find the footprints of a sea god?
2. Where was a village moved to improve the view?
3. Who lost a leg at Waterloo?
4. Where can you find a tea-set waterfall?

Answers on page 187

Northern Ireland

Countryside

There are adventures waiting for you along Northern Ireland's coast with its wonderful scenery, strange cliff shapes, sandy beaches and little fishing harbours to explore.

● Make sure you visit the North Antrim coastline and see Whitepark Bay, a long beach of white sand with caves and fossils to look for. There is a Youth Hostel close to the beach. A little further east is Ballintoy, a tiny harbour where you can watch the fishermen going out in their boats and buy seaweed... to eat!

● If you're feeling brave, visit Carrick-a-Rede. Every summer for over two hundred years fishermen have put up a rope bridge connecting the mainland with a little rocky island 60 feet away. They set their nets to catch the salmon which swim around the north side of the island on their journey to spawn in the rivers Bann and Bush. You can cross the bridge, too, but be careful – it swings and there's a 70-foot drop to the sea below!

174

Off the coast road between Coleraine and Downhill you can visit the ruins of Downhill House and what is left of the eighteenth-century landscaped park created by the remarkable Frederick Hervey, Bishop of Derry (you can find out more about him in the entry on Ickworth in Suffolk). Perched right on the edge of the cliffs is the circular Mussenden Temple which is named after the bishop's cousin. Hervey fitted the temple out as a library and used to spend many hours studying in this wild and isolated spot.

County Antrim

The Giant's Causeway

Bushmills, Co. Antrim BT57 8SU
Tel. Bushmills (026 57) 31582
On B146 Causeway–Dunseverick road

There are many strange legends as to how the Giant's Causeway
was formed. Did warring giants throw the rocks at each other or
was it the home of the Irish giant, Finn McCool? The fact is that
the amazing geometrical rock formations were actually formed
by volcanic action 60 million years ago!

Don't Miss...

● There are lots of wonderful paths to follow along the
coast and up on the cliffs. Let your imagination run wild
and you'll be able to see all sorts of shapes in the rocks: the
Giant's Organ, the Giant's Boot, the Harp are easy ones to
find, but can you make out Finn McCool's granny climbing
the cliffs?

- Sit in the Wishing Chair and make a wish!

- In 1588 some of the ships from the fleeing Spanish Armada tried to get back to Spain by sailing round Ireland's treacherous coast and many were wrecked. You can see the spot where the treasure ship **Girona** sank on the rocks at Port na Spaniagh.

- Visit the visitors' centre to find out more about this stretch of coastline. There is an audio-visual show, displays about the local history and the animal and bird life of the area.

County Down

Castle Ward

Strangford, Downpatrick, Co. Down BT30 7LS
Tel. Strangford (039 686) 204
7m NE of Downspatrick, 1½m W of Strangford village on A25.

Castle Ward is an architectural wonder: one half of the house is built in classical style and the other is gothick. When the house was being built in the 1760s Bernard Ward and his wife Anne couldn't agree on style so decided to meet half way!

Don't Miss...

● The Pastimes Centre where you can dress up in replica Victorian costumes and play with Victorian toys and games.

● The stable yard shows what life would have been like for servants in Victorian times. Visit the stables, the tack-room and the laundry which is packed with equipment and garments of the period.

● This was once a busy agricultural estate and you can still see the waterwheel, corn mill, barn, saw mill and slaughter-house.

● There are lots of grounds to explore; don't miss the birds at Temple Water.

● There is an audio-visual show and display on Strangford Lough in the farmyard.

Mount Stewart

Newtownards, Co. Down BT22 2AD
Tel. Greyabbey (024 774) 387
5m S of Belfast on A20 Newtownards–Portaferry road,
m SE of Newtownards

Mount Stewart was where the nineteenth-century politician,
Lord Castlereagh, grew up. However, the house and garden are
stamped with the personality of a later owner, Lady Edith
Londonderry, the wife of the 7th Marquess, who redecorated
and furnished the house and created the garden you see today.

Don't Miss...

● The Londonderrys socialised with some of the top
social, political and military figures of the day. During the
First World War Lady Edith established the Ark Club, and
many famous people were members. The club would meet
at the couple's London home and every member had a
special name: Winston Churchill was Winnie the Warlock,
Lord Londonderry was Charlie the Cheetah and Lady
Londonderry was Circe the Sorceress. Back in Ireland
Lady Londonderry commissioned sculptures of many of
the figures of the club – the result is the Dodo terrace at
Mount Stewart.

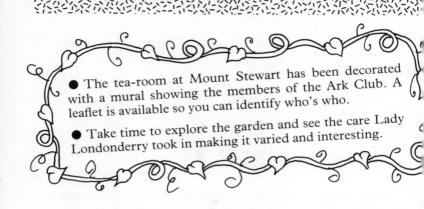

- The tea-room at Mount Stewart has been decorated with a mural showing the members of the Ark Club. A leaflet is available so you can identify who's who.

- Take time to explore the garden and see the care Lady Londonderry took in making it varied and interesting.

Strangford Lough

5,400 acres covering Strangford to Newtownards

Norse adventurers sailing their longboats into this channel called it 'Strong Fiord', which is how the name 'Strangford' came about. The Lough is now a famous marine and wildlife sanctuary with hundreds of different birds and animals to see.

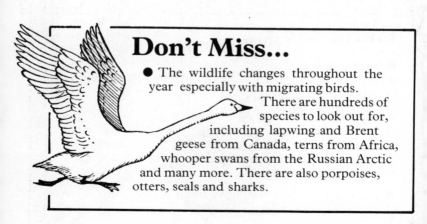

Don't Miss...

- The wildlife changes throughout the year especially with migrating birds. There are hundreds of species to look out for, including lapwing and Brent geese from Canada, terns from Africa, whooper swans from the Russian Arctic and many more. There are also porpoises, otters, seals and sharks.

● There are guided tours given by wardens who point out the bird and wildlife.

● And don't forget the world under the water with its corals, sponges, anemones, crab, starfish and octopus!

County Fermanagh

Florence Court

Near Enniskillen, Co. Fermanagh
Tel. Florencecourt (036 582) 249
8m SW of Enniskillen via A4 and A32 Swanlinbar road

The mid-eighteenth-century house was built for Sir John Cole, set in a 90-acre park and surrounded by mountains.

Don't Miss...

● The service rooms in the basement. The kitchen ceiling is fireproof! The house was badly damaged by fire earlier this century.

● The estate is fascinating and many of its features are being restored. There are lots of things to see like the blacksmith's forge, the water-powered saw mill, the carpenter's workshop, the bark house, ice house, hydraulic ram and eel house.

● Go for one of the walks in the forest park or explore the pleasure grounds and walled garden.

County Londonderry

Springhill

20 Springhill Road, Moneymore, Magherafelt, Co. Londonderry
Tel. Moneymore (064 87) 48210
1m from Moneymore on B18 Moneymore–Coagh road

This fortified manor house was built by settlers from Ayrshire
in Scotland at the end of the seventeenth century. Ten
generations of the Conyngham family have lived at Springhill
and the house still feels like their family home.

Don't Miss...

● The costume collection in the laundry.

● The nursery and collection of old toys.

● The slaughterhouse and turf shed.

● There is an adventure playground
and activities for children are often
arranged. Telephone for more details.

Remember to consult **The National Trust
Handbook** for opening times, admission
prices and other details.

County Tyrone

The Argory

Moy, Dungannon, Co. Tyrone BT71 6NA
Tel. Moy (086 87) 84753
m from Moy, 3m from M1, exit 14

This beautiful Victorian house is in a wonderful setting overlooking the Blackwater River. It was built by Walter McGeogh between 1820 and 1824; his first wife Mary Joy had little time to enjoy it as she sadly died only two years after their wedding in 1826.

Don't Miss...

● The story of the **Birkenhead** in the central corridor. Walter's second son Ralph was on board the steamship when it sank off the Cape of Good Hope in 1852.

● The organ lobby with its superb 1820s barrel organ. The family would have spent many an evening playing or listening to the organ.

● The lovely collection of clothes, hats and shoes from the 1920s belonging to Lady Bond.

● The acetylene gas plant in the Laundry Yard. This provided light for the Argory and was installed in 1906 for the princely sum of £250. You can still see the gas light fittings in the house.

● The coach house with its collection of carriages.

Wellbrook Beetling Mill

20 Wellbrook Road, Corkhill, Cookshill, Co. Tyrone BT80 9RY
Tel. Tulnacross (064 87) 51735
4m W of Cookstown, ½m off A505 Cookstown–Omagh road

This mill gets its name from 'beetling', the process which gives
shiny surface to linen, a cloth for which Ireland is famous. Th
mill has been restored to full working order so you can see, hea
and feel what it was like to work in one of these mills.

Don't Miss...

● The cloth is pounded by hammers called beetles which
are powered by a waterwheel on the end wall of the mill.
Imagine being stuck in the building all day with the loud
thumping noise.

● The mills would have employed children, as appren-
tices, to watch the machines. No scarves or loose clothes
were allowed in case they got caught in the machine and
dragged the worker in!

● There is a display telling the story of the Irish linen
industry.

184

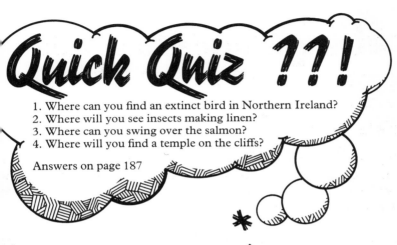

Quick Quiz ??!

1. Where can you find an extinct bird in Northern Ireland?
2. Where will you see insects making linen?
3. Where can you swing over the salmon?
4. Where will you find a temple on the cliffs?

Answers on page 187

Quick Quiz Answers

...von, Berkshire and Buckinghamshire

Pillow mounds at Dolebury Warren.
Dyrham Park.
The Shell Room at Basildon Park.
Claydon House, where Florence Nightingale stayed with her sister.

Cornwall

Trelissick Garden.
Lanhydrock.
Cornish Engines.
Morwenstow.
Trerice.
Cotehele.

Quick Quiz Answers

Devon

1. Baggy Point.
2. The topiary hedge at Knightshayes Court.
3. Lundy.
4. Buckland Abbey, home of Sir Francis Drake.

Gloucestershire

1. Chedworth Roman Villa.
2. Crickley Hill.
3. Snowshill Manor.

Kent and the Isle of Wight

1. Ightham Mote.
2. Chartwell – Jock the cat.
3. Needles Old Battery on the Isle of Wight.

Oxfordshire

Maze solution.

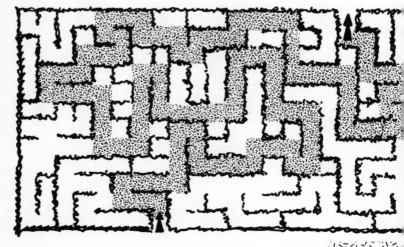

Quick Quiz Answers

Northumberland and Nottinghamshire

Cragside.
Wallington.
Farne Islands.
Clumber Park.

Staffordshire and Suffolk

Melford Hall.
Shugborough.
Mow Cop.
Ickworth.
Moseley Old Hall.

Sussex and Surrey

At Bateman's, Rudyard Kipling's home.
Polesden Lacey.
Major Peter Labellière who asked to be buried upside down on
Box Hill, so that he would be standing on his feet when 'the world
turned upside down' on the day of resurrection.

Wales

On the Whistler mural at Plas Newydd.
Stackpole Estate.
1st Marquess of Anglesey.
The Cup and Saucer folly at Erddig.

Northern Ireland

The Dodo terrace at Mount Stewart.
Wellbrook Beetling Mill.
Carrick-a-Rede rope bridge.
The Mussenden Temple.

Spotter's Guide

Why not use these House Spotter and Countryside Spotter pages to keep your own record of some of the National Trust properties you have visited. Just fill in the sheets after your visit and you'll have a lasting reminder of your day out.

Countryside Spotter

Name of property ―――――――――――――

Location ―――――――――――――――――

Date of visit ―――――――――――――――

Weather conditions ――――――――――――

How far away from home ――――――――――

How long it took to get there ―――――――――

Types of wildflowers and plants seen ――――――

Types of insects seen ―――――――――――

Types of birds and animals seen ――――――――

Marks out of ten for the countryside   10

Draw a picture of something to remind you of your visit

House Spotter

Property visited _____

County _____

Date visited _____

Weather conditions _____

How far away from home _____

How long it took to get there _____

The most interesting thing you saw _____

The most boring thing you saw _____

When was the house built and who for? _____

Draw a picture of something to remind you of your visit

Marks out of ten for the house /10

Marks out of ten for the garden/park /10

Spotter's Guide

Countryside Spotter

Name of property _____

Location _____

Date of visit _____

Weather conditions _____

How far away from home _____

How long it took to get there _____

Types of wildflowers and plants seen _____

Types of insects seen _____

Types of birds and animals seen _____

Marks out of ten for the countryside /10

Draw a picture of something to remind you of your visit

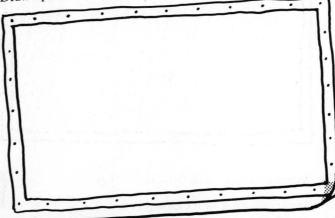

House Spotter

Property visited _____

County _____

Date visited _____

Weather conditions _____

How far away from home _____

How long it took to get there _____

The most interesting thing you saw _____

The most boring thing you saw _____

When was the house built and who for? _____

Draw a picture of something to remind you of your visit

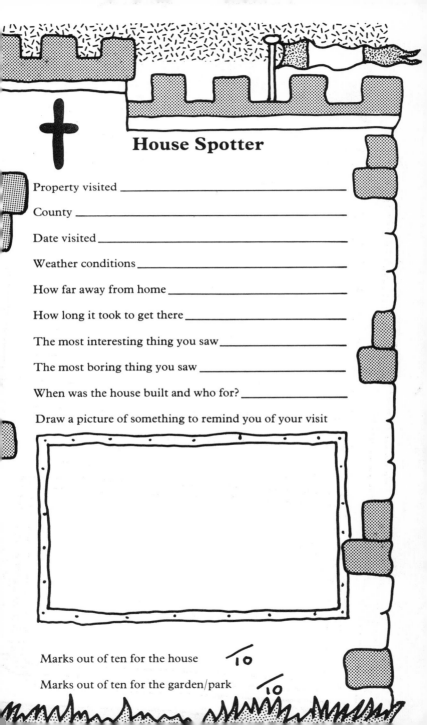

Marks out of ten for the house   10

Marks out of ten for the garden/park   10

Spotter's Guide

Countryside Spotter

Name of property _____

Location _____

Date of visit _____

Weather conditions _____

How far away from home _____

How long it took to get there _____

Types of wildflowers and plants seen _____

Types of insects seen _____

Types of birds and animals seen _____

Marks out of ten for the countryside 10

Draw a picture of something to remind you of your visit

House Spotter

Property visited _____

County _____

Date visited _____

Weather conditions _____

How far away from home _____

How long it took to get there _____

The most interesting thing you saw _____

The most boring thing you saw _____

When was the house built and who for? _____

Draw a picture of something to remind you of your visit

Marks out of ten for the house   10

Marks out of ten for the garden/park   10

Spotter's Guide

Countryside Spotter

Name of property _____

Location _____

Date of visit _____

Weather conditions _____

How far away from home _____

How long it took to get there _____

Types of wildflowers and plants seen _____

Types of insects seen _____

Types of birds and animals seen _____

Marks out of ten for the countryside   10

Draw a picture of something to remind you of your visit

House Spotter

Property visited _____

County _____

Date visited _____

Weather conditions _____

How far away from home _____

How long it took to get there _____

The most interesting thing you saw _____

The most boring thing you saw _____

When was the house built and who for? _____

Draw a picture of something to remind you of your visit

Marks out of ten for the house   /10

Marks out of ten for the garden/park   /10

Spotter's Guide

Countryside Spotter

Name of property _____

Location _____

Date of visit _____

Weather conditions _____

How far away from home _____

How long it took to get there _____

Types of wildflowers and plants seen _____

Types of insects seen _____

Types of birds and animals seen _____

Marks out of ten for the countryside ╱10

Draw a picture of something to remind you of your visit

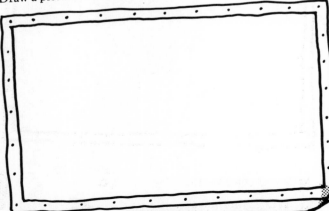

House Spotter

Property visited _____

County _____

Date visited _____

Weather conditions _____

How far away from home _____

How long it took to get there _____

The most interesting thing you saw _____

The most boring thing you saw _____

When was the house built and who for? _____

Draw a picture of something to remind you of your visit

Marks out of ten for the house   10

Marks out of ten for the garden/park   10

Spotter's Guide

Countryside Spotter

Name of property _____

Location _____

Date of visit _____

Weather conditions _____

How far away from home _____

How long it took to get there _____

Types of wildflowers and plants seen _____

Types of insects seen _____

Types of birds and animals seen _____

Marks out of ten for the countryside /10

Draw a picture of something to remind you of your visit

House Spotter

Property visited _____

County _____

Date visited _____

Weather conditions _____

How far away from home _____

How long it took to get there _____

The most interesting thing you saw _____

The most boring thing you saw _____

When was the house built and who for? _____

Draw a picture of something to remind you of your visit

Marks out of ten for the house   10

Marks out of ten for the garden/park   10

Index

This index lists the main property entries together with those counti
with general sections on coast, countryside and minor properties.